IN GOOD COMPANY

Anne Marie Drayton
Charles Skidmore

 Addison-Wesley Publishing Company

A Publication of the World Language Division

Anne Marie Drayton is an ESL teacher in the Boston, Massachusetts, schools.

Charles Skidmore is an ESL teacher in the Boston, Massachusetts, schools and is co-author of *Skill Sharpeners 1, 2, 3,* and *4,* also published by Addison-Wesley.

Acknowledgments

Editorial: Elly Schottman, Talbot F. Hamlin

Production/Manufacturing: James W. Gibbons

Photographs: p. 1, A.W. Bentley, courtesy of National Oceanographic and Atmospheric Administration; p. 45, Carlos Bartels; p. 54, courtesy New York Convention and Visitor's Bureau; p. 97, courtesy American Telephone and Telegraph Company; p. 108, Leonard Lee Rue, III. All other photographs by George Mastellone.

Other illustrations: Laura Maine

Cover and Text design: Bonnie Chayes Yousefian

ISBN 0-201-16409-4
18 19 20 21 22 23 24 25-CRS-0201009998

INTRODUCTION

In Good Company is an integrated skill-building reader for low intermediate to intermediate students of English as a second language. Each of its fifteen units includes a chapter in a continuous fiction story, a related nonfiction reading, and a variety of exercises to build reading comprehension, vocabulary, grammar, and other language skills. The program is structured cumulatively so that each skill is reused, reviewed, and reinforced after its introduction.

The fiction readings are built around a classroom in a school called The English Learning Center and its teacher and students. Some of the readings are centered on the teacher, others on certain of the students. The varied subjects and situations relate directly to experiences and concerns that many ESL students share: a parent who speaks no English and can't ask directions, a student who is unwilling to use her English language skills; a teacher who lets his past social failures affect his present actions, for example. Both students and teachers are portrayed as fellow human beings with thoughts and feelings not very different from the reader's.

The nonfiction readings relate thematically to the fiction chapters. Thus when the fiction chapter concerns the missing mother of one of the students, the nonfiction reading is about missing persons; when a mystery (missing theater tickets) is solved by one of the students in the fiction reading, the related nonfiction essay is on Sherlock Holmes.

Each unit includes both literal and inferential comprehension questions, structured in such a way as to give students practice in producing the target grammatical structures used in the reading. The inferential questions encourage students to go beyond the facts of the story and express their own opinions and emotional reactions to the events described. Answers to the questions may be written on composition paper or in a notebook or, at your option, given orally and discussed in the class.

The nonfiction readings, while related thematically to the fiction passages and written in the same tense, are somewhat more difficult in vocabulary and concepts. Comprehension questions check student understanding of the readings, and the target reading skills are applied to them. Brief reviews of skills taught in earlier units are included in this section. The units end with sections designed specifically to build and reinforce speaking and writing skills, "Talking About You" and "Composition Corner." Questions in "Talking About You" encourage students to express their own ideas, opinions, and feelings and to describe personal experiences and events related to the theme of the unit. Questions in "Composition Corner" are applicative in nature, taking the student beyond the readings to a consideration and extension of some of the concepts presented in them.

The target reading skills are listed in the Table of Contents following the titles of the fiction and nonfiction readings. Grammar skills are not listed, since they consist mainly of use of specific tenses. The present and present progressive tenses are used throughout Units 1 through 4; in Unit 4, the present progressive is used with a future implication. The simple past is used in Units 5 and 6, and the simple past and past continuous in Units 7 through 10. The present perfect is introduced in Unit 11 and used through the rest of the book.

While speaking and writing skills are developed in each unit, the emphasis throughout *In Good Company* is on reading. Students in classroom tests of the material were enthusiastic about the stories and eager to discuss them; they attempted the exercises without hesitation. The nonfiction readings were especially popular, and catch phrases from them came up repeatedly throughout the year. Most importantly, quarterly and final testing showed that the students retained the vocabulary and skills introduced in the program.

CONTENTS

* These sections are perforated and may be removed before the book is used, if desired.

1. FIRST WITH THE NEWS

Sometimes it's fun to be first with the news. Here's a story about a student who wants to be the first to tell something. Read the story and see if he is.

It is 9:00 on a cold, windy morning in late December. Otto Fox and his students are in their classroom at the English Learning Center. Outside the wind is blowing, and the sky is gray.

George isn't doing his work. He's looking out the window. It's beginning to snow. George is excited. He wants to tell Mr. Fox and the other students about the snow. All the students in this class are from warm places. It never snows in their countries. Everyone wants to see snow, and George wants to be first with the news.

George has a problem. He doesn't remember the English word for snow. George gets out his bilingual dictionary, and he looks for the word in his own language. He's nervous. He looks at the other students. He wants to be first. He's thinking, "Please don't look out the window. Please don't see the snow." At last George finds the word. It's "SNOW." George is ready to say the magic word. He opens his mouth.

"Look, it's beginning to snow," says Mr. Fox. The students all turn and look out the window.

George closes his mouth. He thinks, "I hate snow!"

What's in the Story?

Answer these questions about "First with the News." Use complete sentences and write on your own paper. You can find the answers in the story.

1. What month is it?
2. What is the weather like?
3. Who is Otto Fox?
4. Who is George?
5. George looks out of the window. What does he see?
6. Where do the students in the classroom come from?
7. What is George's problem?
8. What book helps George?
9. Who says, "It's beginning to snow"?

What Do You Think?

Answer these questions. Use the story and your own ideas. Write on your own paper.

1. What season is it? How do you know?
2. Is George a good student? Why or why not?
3. Why does George need to know the word for snow in English?
4. What language does George speak? Does the story tell you?
5. Does George *really* hate snow? Explain your answer.

What Happens First?

Sequence is the order in which things happen. When you complete a sequence exercise, you show what happened first, what happened next, and so on. Here are some sequence exercises.

A. How well do you remember "First with the News"? On your paper, write the sentences in the order in which they happened.

   a. George sees the snow.
   b. Mr. Fox tells the class about the snow.
   c. George looks out the window.
   d. George looks in his dictionary.
   e. George isn't doing his work.

B. Here are activities you or your friends do often. Think about how you do them. On your paper, write the sentences in the correct sequence.

Giving a Party

   a. Clean up after the party
   b. Prepare the food
   c. Decide whom to invite
   d. Invite people
   e. Everyone has a good time
   f. Decide to have a party
   g. Buy the food

Buying Clothes

   a. Try it on
   b. Decide to buy it
   c. Take it home
   d. Go to the store
   e. Pay for it
   f. Look in the mirror
   g. Find something you like

Sending a Letter

   a. Write the letter
   b. Put a stamp on the envelope
   c. Write the address
   d. Walk to the mailbox
   e. Get a pen and paper
   f. Drop the letter in the mailbox
   g. Put the letter in an envelope

Taking a Shower

   a. Turn on the water
   b. Get out of the shower
   c. Get undressed
   d. Dry yourself
   e. Wash yourself
   f. Get dressed
   g. Get into the shower

C. Read the following sentences. Notice words like *then, first, next,* and *finally.* These words can help you arrange the sentences in the right order. On your paper, write the sentences in the correct sequence.

   1. **a.** After his bus ride, he gets on the train.
   b. Mr. Chan leaves his house at 7:00 A.M.
   c. Then he rides the train for five stops.
   d. He finally arrives at his office at 8:15.
   e. He gets off the train and walks upstairs to work.
   f. He rides the bus for 2 miles.
   g. He walks to the bus stop.

2. a. Then make the salad dressing.
    b. Dry them and cut or tear them into smaller pieces.
    c. Next, put the pieces in a large bowl.
    d. Begin with beautiful fresh vegetables.
    e. Just before dinner, pour the dressing over the salad.
    f. Wash them in cold water.

3. a. Her last class is woodworking on the first floor.
    b. Wanda finally leaves school at 2:15.
    c. She goes to her first four classes on the second floor.
    d. Then she goes to gym for 5th and 6th period.
    e. Wanda Jimenez begins school at 7:45.
    f. After her 4th period class she goes to lunch.

*Every student likes to be first with the news
if the news is . . .*

NO SCHOOL TODAY!

During the winter in the cold areas of the United States, there are no classes when there is a heavy snowfall. This is because the snow falls on the roads, and it is difficult for cars and buses to run. The streets are slippery, and accidents can happen. Sometimes the wind, ice, or snow breaks the electric lines. Then schools, houses, and offices lose their electricity. Schools almost always close when there is no electricity.

When there is a storm, students and their parents watch television or listen to the radio to hear the news about school closings. The superintendent of the school calls the radio or television station and tells if the school is closed for the day. Many students are happy to have an extra holiday.

Information, Please

Use facts from "No School Today!" and your own knowledge and ideas. Write your answers on your piece of paper.

1. Give three reasons why there is no school after a heavy snowfall.
2. How do the students and teachers know when there is no school?

3. Write five things you cannot do when there is no electricity.
4. Name two other times when there are no classes in your school.

What Happens Next?

On your paper, write the sentences in the correct sequence.

a. The superintendent decides to close the schools.
b. The snow covers the roads.
c. The children are happy because they have a day off.
d. The snow begins to fall.
e. Parents and students listen to the radio and television.
f. The roads become slippery.
g. The superintendent calls the radio and television stations.

Talking about You

1. Do you like to be first with the news? Why or why not?

2. What is the weather like in your country?

3. Does it snow where you live now? If not, are there any other reasons why they cancel classes in your area? What are these reasons?

Composition Corner

1. Can you tell George's story in your own words? Think about the story, then write a summary of "First with the News."

2. What do you do on a day off from school? Write about your activities from the time you get up until you go to sleep. Think about the correct order when you write your story.

2. THE LETTER

The next story is a letter. Read it and see what one student writes to her friend back home.

It is night. Maria is writing a letter to her friend back home in her own country. The friend is learning English too. Here is the letter.

Dear Rita,

How are you? I am fine. I miss you and all our friends at

school. I miss our country's warm weather, too. It is freezing here. There are five inches of snow on the ground! The snow is pretty on the first day, but on the second day it is all black and dirty. In English they call the dirty, wet snow "slush." I hate it, and I hate the cold.

But I love school. I go to a school called the English Learning Center. It is a school for students who are new to the United States. All the classes are in English. The teachers are friendly, and they do a good job.

My favorite class is English. It is a very small class. There are only eight students: four boys, George, Alain, Juan, and Tin-Sek, and three other girls, Trang, Ahmad, and Juli. Our teacher is funny. His name is Otto Fox. I think he is in his early thirties. He is very nice, but a little "nervous." He likes us to speak in class—but not too loudly. He likes us to have fun—but not too much. And he likes us to be on time, but he is often late himself.

The students come from all different parts of the world. We have to speak English or no one understands anyone else. I am never embarrassed to speak because the class is small and Mr. Fox is nice. He never yells at us if we make a mistake. When the students talk to each other during class he says it's a good thing that English has lots of words because we have a lot to say. That is his idea of a joke. Ha! Ha!

Well, I have to go study. I have an algebra test tomorrow. I miss you, and I miss home. I remember all the good times. Please write soon. Sometimes I feel alone here.

Love,

Maria

What's in the Story?

Answer these questions about "The Letter." Use complete sentences, and write on your own paper. You can find the answers in the story.

1. Who is Maria writing to?
2. What does Maria miss about her own country?
3. What is "slush"?
4. What kind of students go to the English Learning Center?
5. What are the teachers like at the English Learning Center?
6. What is Maria's favorite class?
7. Why do the students have to speak English in class?
8. Why isn't Maria embarrassed to speak in class?
9. What does Mr. Fox say when the students talk too much?
10. How old is Otto Fox?

What Do You Think?

Answer these questions. Use the story and your own ideas. Write on your own paper.

1. Why is Maria writing in English?
2. What is the weather like in Maria's country?
3. Describe Otto Fox's personality.
4. How does Maria feel about the other students?
5. What does she think of Otto Fox's jokes?
6. How does Maria feel about her new home?

How Are They Alike?

A category is the name of a group of things that have something in common. When you categorize a list of words, you are telling how all the words in the list are similar—how each one is the same as the others. For example, apples and grapes look and taste different, but they both belong to the category "fruit." Canada and Mexico both belong to the category "countries in North America."

Look at each list of words below. Decide how all the items on the list are the same. On your own paper, write a label or title that describes the five words on each list. This title is the category. For example, the first list can be labeled: 1. *Parts of the face.*

1. chin
cheek
nose
forehead
eyes

2. carrots
beans
broccoli
lettuce
cabbage

3. algebra
history
biology
chemistry
geography

4. dictionary
atlas
encyclopedia
almanac
In Good Company

5. brother
sister
uncle
cousin
father

6. niece
grandmother
daughter
aunt
sister

7. goldfish
hamster
parakeet
dog
cat

8. school
museum
library
hospital
church

9. monkey
horse
goat
lion
cow

10. aspirin
    sugar
    teeth
    snow
    milk

11. English
    French
    Spanish
    Mexican
    American

12. juice
    gasoline
    cola
    milk
    water

13. Atlantic
    Pacific
    Mississippi
    Gulf of Mexico
    Caribbean

14. music
    voices
    fire alarm
    thunder
    doorbell

15. tree
    cell
    zoo
    glass
    jazz

What's the Message?

The main idea of a paragraph is the idea or message that the author wants the reader to know and understand. To find the main idea, you have to read the paragraph and decide what subject or idea all the sentences have in common, what message they all send or give support to. For example, look at the following sentences: *Chickens give us eggs. Dogs work with sheep. Cows give milk. Dogs help blind people to find their way.* All these sentences help to prove one idea. This idea is that animals help people in many different ways. If these sentences were a paragraph, that would be the main idea of the paragraph.

Now read each of the following paragraphs. When you finish reading a paragraph, think about the message of the paragraph. Then, on your paper, answer the question about the main idea.

1. People do many kinds of work in hospitals. Everyone knows about doctors and nurses, but there are many other hospital careers. Physical therapists help people to exercise injured parts of their bodies. X-ray technicians take x-ray photographs of patients. Nurse's Aides help the nurses to take care of the patients.

   The main idea of this paragraph is:

   a. Doctors work in hospitals.

   b. Nurse's Aides help people.

   c. Hospitals are places for sick people.

   d. Hospitals have many kinds of jobs.

The Letter 9

2. When people talk about the Romance languages, they aren't talking about love or romance at all. They are talking about a group of modern languages that come from an older language. The major Romance languages are Italian, Spanish, French, and Portuguese. People call these languages *Romance* languages because they all come from Latin, the language of the *Romans*.

The main idea of this paragraph is:

a. The Romance languages are about love and romance.
b. The Romance languages come from Latin, the language of the Romans.
c. The Romance languages are Italian, Spanish, French, and Portuguese.
d. People don't speak Latin any more; they speak the Romance languages.

3. Fast-food restaurants—restaurants where you can get something to eat quickly—are very popular in the United States. Many people like fast-food restaurants because they are so fast. There is little or no waiting. Other people like them because they are cheap. Large families especially like the fact that these restaurants are not expensive. There is no tipping in a fast-food restaurant, either. There is no waiter or waitress, so there is no reason to leave any extra money behind. Of course, many people just like the food.

The main idea of this paragraph is:

a. Fast-food restaurants are not expensive.
b. There are thousands of fast-food restaurants in the United States.
c. There are many reasons why Americans eat at fast-food restaurants.
d. Fast-food restaurants are fast.

4. There are many important awards for actors and actresses in the United States. The three most popular awards are the Oscar, the Tony, and the Emmy. The Oscar is an award for excellence in movies. It is probably the most famous of the three awards, because people all over the world watch the presentation of the Oscars on television every year. The Tony award is an important award for people in the New York theater. The winners of the Tony award are the best actors and actresses on Broadway, the theater capital of the United States. Finally, there is the Emmy. The Emmy is an award for the best actors and actresses in television. Many Americans watch the Emmy award show to see which of their favorite television personalities win the award as the best actor and actress of the year.

The main idea of this paragraph is:

a. The Tony award is for the theater.
b. Television actors receive the Emmy award for good acting.
c. Millions of people around the world know about the Oscars.
d. The Oscar, Tony, and Emmy are three important awards for American actors.

5. In every large city, there are neighborhoods where immigrants keep their languages and traditions alive. In New York City there is "Little Italy." Many people there speak Italian and celebrate festivals from the old country. In Miami's "Little Havana," Cuban culture is very evident, and you can hear Spanish on the street and see shop windows full of advertisements in Spanish. Many cities have a neighborhood called Chinatown. There are many Chinese restaurants and businesses in these neighborhoods. People are proud of their customs and traditions. They keep them alive in their neighborhoods.

The main idea of this paragraph is:

a. There are many neighborhoods in large cities.

b. Many immigrants keep their culture and language alive in ethnic neighborhoods.

c. "Little Italy" is a neighborhood in New York City where people celebrate festivals from the old country.

d. Many immigrants live in large cities.

Mr. Fox says that English is a big language.
Read about . . .

ENGLISH

English is a big language. It has the largest vocabulary of any language in the world. There are more than 800,000 words in the English language. About 300,000 of these are technical words. Scientists, doctors, and lawyers use these technical words in their work. Every job has its special vocabulary. The technical words of plumbers, mechanics, computer programmers, and airline pilots help to make English such a large language. No one uses or knows all of the words in English! The average adult knows and uses about 65,000 words.

More than 300,000,000 people speak English as their native language. Most people in the United States, Canada, England, Ireland, Scotland, Wales, Australia, and New Zealand speak English as their first or native language. Millions of other people around the world speak English as a second language.

Many people learn English when they come to live in English-speaking countries. Other people learn English in their own countries. They use English when they do business or when they travel. There are many students who learn English for fun and pleasure. They want to read books, magazines, and newspapers printed in English, or to understand the actors in English, American, and Australian movies. People study English for many reasons, and they all learn quickly that it is a big language.

It's a big job to learn English well, but if you can read this article, you are already on your way to success in English.

Information, Please

Use facts from the reading and your own knowledge and ideas. Write your answers on a separate piece of paper.

1. About how many words are there in the English language?
2. About how many words does the average English speaker know?
3. Who uses special vocabulary?
4. About how many people speak English as their native language?
5. In what countries do people speak English as their first language?
6. Give three reasons why people learn English.

What's the Message?

What is the main idea of this reading? Write your answer on your own paper.

a. There are many people in the world who speak English.
b. People learn English for many different reasons.
c. English is a big language.
d. There are many technical words in English.

Talking about You

1. In what country or countries do people speak your native language?

2. What do you miss about your country?

3. Do you know any other languages besides your native language and English? Which ones? How and why did you learn them?

4. Do you want to learn any other languages? Why or why not?

Composition Corner

1. Write a letter to a friend back home in your country. Talk about your new life here and the things you miss back home.

2. List ten ways in which the United States is different from your country. After you make your list, put the information in the form of a paragraph.

3. THE SUPERVISOR

Some people always come late. Others are always early. Read this story to see what happens when a teacher is late.

7:30
Ms. Goodwin

It is morning. Otto Fox wakes up. "Oh no!" he says. "It's 7:00! I'm late. What a day to be late! The new supervisor is coming."

Otto hurries to the bathroom. He takes a quick shower and shaves. "Why don't I have a beard?" he thinks. Finally, he gets dressed. Otto is ready to run out of the house, but he hears "arf, arf." "Oh, Sandy, I can't forget you," he says. "Here's your food. Be a good boy. Mrs. Clark is coming to take you out at 8:30."

It's 7:25. Otto leaves the house and runs to the bus stop. "Where's the bus? Where's the bus?" Otto thinks. He looks at his watch—7:30. Otto looks down the street and sees a taxi. He decides to take it. He waves his arm and the taxi stops. Otto gets into the taxi and says, "English Learning Center—fast!"

"Sure, boss," says the driver. "What's your hurry?"

"I'm late for class, and my supervisor is coming today."

"Don't worry. We can be there in ten minutes."

"Terrific!" says Otto. "But be careful. I don't like to go too fast in a car."

"Don't worry. I'm a good driver."

"I'm glad . . . Hey! Look out for that dog!"

"Don't worry, Teach! He's a mile away."

"A mile away? Do you need glasses?"

"Relax. We're almost there," says the driver. "Tell me about the supervisor. What's he like?"

"Not he. *She*. I don't really know her well, but she seems nice. . . . But her reports go downtown, and if I'm late . . ."

"Oh, go on. Late one time. That doesn't matter."

"Well, you see, I'm late a lot," says Otto.

"You're not too late today. Here we are at the English Learning Center. That's $4.00."

"Great. Thanks." He hands the driver $5.00. "Keep the change."

Otto enters the school through the front door. He runs up the stairs to his room. He looks at his watch. It's 7:42. "Twelve minutes late. Not too bad." He walks into the classroom. "There she is," he thinks. "Why can't she be late?"

Ms. Goodwin sees Mr. Fox and smiles. "Good morning, Mr. Fox. How are you?"

"Fine, thank you, Ms. Goodwin. A little late, I'm afraid. My car is giving me some trouble."

The students smile at each other. They know that Mr. Fox doesn't have a car and that he is late a lot.

Ms. Goodwin says, "I'm here to watch the class, Mr. Fox. Please begin your lesson."

At the end of the class, Ms. Goodwin says to the students, "This is an excellent class!" Then she turns to Mr. Fox and says, "I want to talk to you later today."

Mr. Fox says, "Fine, let's have coffee after school."

Ms. Goodwin smiles. "3:00," she says. "Don't be late."

What's in the Story?

Answer these questions about "The Supervisor." Use complete sentences and write on your own paper. You can find the answers in the story.

1. What time does Otto Fox get up?
2. Why is Otto upset?
3. What does Otto do to get ready to go to work?
4. What time does Otto arrive at the bus stop?
5. How much does the taxi ride cost?
6. How much is the tip that Otto gives the driver?
7. Who arrives at the classroom first, Otto or the supervisor?
8. What is the supervisor's name?
9. What time do Mr. Fox and the supervisor plan to meet?
10. Where do they plan to meet?

What Do You Think?

Answer these questions. Use the story and your own ideas. Write on your own paper.

1. Otto says, "Why don't I have a beard?" What does he mean?
2. Is the bus stop close to Otto's house? How do you know?
3. Who is Sandy?
4. Who is Mrs. Clark?
5. What is the taxi driver like?
6. Is the taxi driver a good driver? How do you know?
7. Why does Otto say that his car is giving him trouble?
8. What time does school begin at the English Learning Center?
9. Why does the supervisor say, "3:00. Don't be late."?
10. Do the students like Mr. Fox? How do you know?

Supporting Details

Supporting details prove or explain why a main idea is true. For example, a main idea statement might be, "Mr. Fox is very busy in the morning." You can prove this is true if you describe specific things that Mr. Fox does each morning. Some of these things are: he has to shower, he has to shave, he has to dress, he has to feed his dog, he has to walk to the bus stop. These statements prove that Mr. Fox is busy in the morning. They support the main idea.

Following are some main idea statements. For each one, write five specific examples that prove or explain why each main idea statement is true. Use complete sentences and write on separate paper. The first one is done for you.

1. People write many letters each year.

    a. They want to send news to their families.

    b. They want to keep close to their families.

    c. They want to find out some information.

    d. They want to answer an advertisement in a newspaper.

    e. They want to complain to a politician or government agency.

2. Weekends are busy times for many people.
3. People move to other countries for many reasons.
4. Today, a large number of students plan to go to college.
5. Many things make people laugh.
6. There are important qualities that make good students stand out.

Support the Main Idea

Here are some more main idea statements. Below each statement are five or six sentences. Some of the sentences help to prove or explain the main idea; others do not. In the first example, the main idea is, "Mr. Fox is a good teacher." The statements, "His classes are interesting," "He always prepares his classes," and "He cares about his students" all support the main idea that Mr. Fox is a good teacher. The other statements are true, but they do not support the main idea statement.

Now read the other main idea statements. On your paper, write the statements that support the main idea. For the first item, write: b. His classes are interesting. c. He cares about his students. d. He always prepares his classes.

1. Mr. Fox is a good teacher.

    a. He is almost always late.
    b. His classes are interesting.
    c. He cares about his students.
    d. He always prepares his classes.
    e. He comes to school by bus.

2. Pets can make a person's life happier.

    a. They provide company and friendship.
    b. They give people a chance for physical contact.
    c. They need food and water.
    d. They are fun to play with.
    e. They love their owners without question.
    f. They go to the veterinarian once a year.

3. Cigarette smoking is unhealthy.

   a. It causes lung cancer.
   b. It is a very expensive habit.
   c. It increases the chance of heart disease.
   d. It can burn holes in carpets.
   e. It can harm unborn babies.
   f. It causes emphysema and other respiratory problems.

4. Electricity is important in everyday life.

   a. Thomas Edison invented the electric light bulb.
   b. Electricity lights up city streets and houses at night.
   c. Electricity brings entertainment to our homes through TV and radio.
   d. Electricians are people who take care of problems with electricity.
   e. Electricity makes it possible for people to see at night.
   f. Electricity heats and cools many houses and apartments.

5. There are many ways to find money to go to college.

   a. The federal government awards educational grants to students.
   b. It is very expensive to go to college.
   c. Many states give college scholarships to students.
   d. Part-time jobs and summer jobs are ways to earn money for college.
   e. Some parents can't afford to pay college expenses.

Mr. Fox lies in the story to get himself out of trouble. Read about other reasons that people tell . . .

WHITE LIES

Very often, newborn babies are not beautiful. They are wrinkled or bald, or they have an angry expression on their faces that seems to say, "Go away! I hate everybody." But to a parent, that bald, wrinkled, mean-faced baby is the most beautiful and perfect child in the world. When that proud father or mother asks you, "Well, what do you think—isn't she beautiful?" what are you going to say? Is this the time for the truth? Of course not!

You look that proud father in the eye and say, "Yes, she is! She's a real beauty. She's one in a million. She's going to be a movie star! I can tell! She's as pretty as a picture."

This is what we call in English a white lie. White lies don't hurt people; they aren't cruel or angry words. People use them to make a difficult situation a little easier. When people refuse dates, forget their homework, or taste something new that they don't especially like while eating at a friend's house, they tell a white lie. They are trying to be kind. They don't want to hurt someone's feelings. It is important to be honest. But many people feel that being kind and considerate is sometimes more important.

Information, Please

Use facts from the reading and your own knowledge and ideas to answer these questions. Use complete sentences, and write on your own paper.

1. How do some newborn babies look?
2. How do babies look to their parents?
3. What is a white lie?
4. Why do people tell white lies?

What's the Message?

On your paper, write the sentence that gives the main idea of this reading.

a. Babies are beautiful only to their parents.
b. It is important to be honest at all times.
c. People tell white lies to be considerate.
d. White lies aren't cruel words.

Supporting Details

Now list on your paper five statements that prove or explain the main idea statement that you chose in "What's the Message."

Talking about You

Discuss these questions in class.

1. Are you usually early or late? Why or why not?

2. How do you feel when people are too early or too late for a meeting or appointment with you?

3. Do you ever tell white lies? If you do, and if you can remember the exact situation, tell about it.

Composition Corner

1. Otto has to feed Sandy, and someone has to come and take him for a walk. Write a composition about the responsibilities of owning a pet. What are the things you have to do for a pet when you care for one?

2. Mr. Fox's cab driver is an out-of-the-ordinary person. Describe a person in your own life who is out of the ordinary, someone who is interesting and fun to be with. It can be anyone. It can be someone in your family, someone you work with, or someone that you know in school.

4. STRAWBERRY

People can change in many different ways. Read this story and see how and why a girl named Trang changes.

"You need to practice your English, Trang. You don't speak enough. You can read and write well, but I never hear you talk."

"Yes, Mr. Fox," she says. But she's thinking, "I don't know anyone to talk to. My family does not speak English. We only speak our own language at home. I want to practice my English, but I am afraid to speak in class. The other students know more English."

The bell rings. Trang leaves and begins to walk home alone. She looks in the windows of the supermarket and the other stores. She can read all the signs and can name all the things in the windows.

She looks at the big signs in the supermarket window. "Milk," she reads, "$.95, Rice $.89, paper towels, special, 2 for $1.00, strawberries..." She stops. "Strawberries!" she says. "How I love strawberries! But they are so expensive."

Trang turns the corner. She sees a skinny, little kitten. "This kitten is always here, always looking for food," she thinks. "It doesn't have a home."

Suddenly, a man throws a rock at the kitten. "That cat is breaking the garbage bags again," he says. "This time, I'm going to kill it."

Trang runs to the kitten and picks it up. "No!" she says. She's angry. "This is my cat," she says to the man. "Don't you hurt it! It's just hungry. I'm going to take it home."

"So take it home," says the man. "Good. I never want to see that cat again."

Trang runs home. She feels nervous and afraid, but she also feels happy. She looks at her kitten and says, "I do know English! I can speak and people understand me."

At home, she thinks, "I'm going to practice English more now. I know I can speak with the other students in class. And I'm going to talk to this cat only in English. I'm going to give it an American name to remind myself to practice. I know! I'm going to call it Strawberry."

What's in the Story?

Answer these questions about "Strawberry." Use complete sentences and write on your own paper. You can find the answers in the story.

1. What does Mr. Fox tell Trang to do?
2. Does Trang speak English with her family? Why or why not?
3. Why doesn't Trang practice her English more in class?
4. How does Trang get home from school?
5. What does Trang look at in the store window?
6. Why is the man angry at the kitten?
7. Why is Trang angry with the man?
8. What does Trang do with the cat?
9. Why does Trang give the cat an American name?
10. What does Trang name the cat? Why?

What Do You Think?

Answer these questions. Use the story and your own ideas. Write on your paper.

1. What is Trang like?
2. What is the man like?
3. Why is the kitten breaking the garbage bags?
4. Trang is afraid to speak English. Why does she speak English to the man?
5. How does Trang know the man understands her?
6. Why is Trang nervous and happy at the same time?

Predicting Outcomes

An outcome is a result or an ending. For example, if you miss the last 30 seconds of a very exciting basketball game because your television breaks down, you can call up a friend and ask the outcome of the game. You want to know who the winners are. In the exercise below, you have to read each paragraph and predict a possible outcome of it. You can't be sure what is going to happen, of course, but there is enough information in each paragraph to give you some good ideas about what will happen.

Remember that you can't tell for certain what people are going to do. So don't be surprised if other students write outcomes that are different from yours.

The first answer is done for you. Use it as an example for the others. Write your answers on separate paper.

1. Trang feels bad about her English. She speaks to the man and he understands her. What do you think is the outcome? Possible Outcome: *Trang is going to speak English more in the future.*

2. John loves to drive his car fast. One day a child runs into the street. John almost hits her. What do you think is the outcome?

3. Tin-Sek has a test on Monday. Sunday night there is a good movie on television. Tin-Sek decides to watch the movie. He doesn't study. He fails the test. What do you think is the outcome?

4. Mike has a secret. He tells his best friend Joe about the secret. Mike says, "Don't tell anyone, Joe." But Joe tells John and John tells everyone else. Mike is furious with Joe. What do you think is the outcome?

5. Clark doesn't like science. He thinks it's boring. This year, there is a new science teacher. This teacher loves science, and her classes are interesting and exciting. She talks about how science works in everyday life. What do you think is the outcome?

6. Jeffrey depends on his brother to wake him up in the morning. Sometimes his brother wakes up late or forgets to get Jeffrey up on time. Jeffrey's boss is angry because Jeffrey is late so often. What do you think is the outcome?

7. Lucy often forgets things. She forgets appointments and birthdays and homework assignments. She forgets to pay the telephone bill, and the company turns off her telephone service. She misses an important phone call. What do you think is the outcome?

8. Jenny thinks that nobody likes her. She doesn't talk or smile in class because she is afraid that no one wants to talk to her. One day she sees a classmate trying to carry a large box. "Do you need some help?" asks Jenny. The classmate smiles and says, "Thanks Jenny. That's very nice of you. Help me carry the box to the cafeteria. Maybe we can have a soda and talk." What do you think is the outcome?

9. Roger is always complaining. "I don't like this." "I don't like that." "This is bad." "I don't like her." "This is boring." "This is stupid." "This is difficult." "This is too easy." One day Roger's friend says, "Roger, don't you like anything? It's no fun to talk to you." What do you think is the outcome?

10. Randy's dog is very destructive. He runs around the neighborhood, digs up the flowers, and chases the mail carrier. Randy's neighbors call the police. Randy is very embarrassed. What do you think is the outcome?

More about Outcomes

When you predict the outcome of a situation, you look at what is happening at the moment and make a decision about what is going to happen. For example, if you are outside and the wind starts to blow and dark clouds appear in the sky, you know that it is time to get indoors. You know that it is probably going to rain. You are predicting an outcome.

Look at the matching exercise below. Column A tells you about certain things that are happening at the present time. Column B lists possible outcomes or predictions. Think about what is happening in each situation in Column A and match it with the correct outcome in Column B. Write the answers on your paper. For example, for the first item, write: *1. The cat's going to run away when it sees her.*

Column A

1. Baby Candice always pulls the cat's tail.

2. Ming's older sisters are afraid of dogs.

3. Paul's puppy always runs into the street.

4. Jeanne says the same words to her parrot every day.

5. Debbie gets nervous and jumps around when a bee gets near her.

6. Grandma Nugent is beginning to keep chickens in her backyard.

7. Factories are polluting the river.

8. Pandora the cat likes to explore people's garages and basements.

9. It is against the law to hunt or kill an American bald eagle.

10. Nobody knows that the door of the hamsters' cage is open.

Column B

a. He's going to be hit by a car someday.

b. One is going to sting her someday.

c. He's going to learn to repeat the words.

d. She's going to get locked in some night.

e. One of them is going to escape.

f. Some fish are going to die.

g. The eagle population is going to grow.

h. She's going to have fresh eggs every week.

i. The cat's going to run away when it sees her.

j. She is going to learn to be afraid of dogs, too.

Now that Strawberry has a home, she probably spends a lot of time . . .

CATNAPPING

Cats sleep about 2/3 of each day. Kittens, sick cats, and old cats sleep more than healthy adult cats, but all cats love to sleep at any time of the day or night. People usually sleep a single session of six to eight hours, but cats prefer to take many short sleep periods. Because of this, we call the short naps that people take "catnaps."

Many times cats adjust their sleeping schedule so that they are awake when their owners are home and want to play with them. When cats are alone and bored, they take naps.

Cats probably dream just as people do. Perhaps in the future, scientists can discover what cats dream about. For now, we can only guess.

One thing is certain. Almost everyone loves to sleep, but cats are the sleep champions!

Information, Please

Use facts from the reading and your own knowledge and ideas. Write your answers on a separate piece of paper.

1. How many hours do cats sleep each day? (You're going to have to do some arithmetic.)
2. About how many hours do most people sleep during the night?
3. What is a catnap?
4. Why do cats like to stay awake when their owners are home?
5. Why are cats called "the sleep champions"?

What's the Message?

What is the main idea of this reading? Write your answer on your own paper.

a. Everybody loves to sleep.
b. A normal cat sleeps most of the day.
c. Most Americans like to catnap.
d. Scientists are studying what cats dream about.

Predicting Outcomes

Read the paragraph below. What do you think is going to happen when the nurse changes her work schedule? Write your answer on a separate piece of paper.

A nurse who usually works during the daytime has to work at night for the next few months. The night shift at the hospital is from 11:00 p.m. to 7:00 a.m. How do you think the nurse's schedule and her cat's schedule are going to change? Think about their sleeping, eating, and playing schedules.

Talking about You

1. Do you have a pet? What kind of pet is it? What is it like?

2. If you have a pet, tell the class why your pet is important to you and how your life is different because of your pet. If you don't have a pet, tell the class your feelings about animals. If you are afraid of animals, tell why.

3. Think of something or someone in your life that changed you. Talk about who or what it was and what happened.

Composition Corner

1. Dreams can be about what we like best or what we are afraid of most. Think about what cats like to do and what they are afraid of. Write a composition that describes a cat's dream.

2. Are you an "early bird" or a "night owl"? Do you like to go to bed early and get up at dawn, or would you rather stay up late and then sleep until noon? Maybe you like to get up early, stay up late, and catnap in between. Write about your favorite waking and sleeping schedule and tell why you like it.

5. VALENTINE'S DAY

Sometimes memories of the past can make us unhappy in the present. Read the next story and see how this happens to Otto Fox.

It is February 13th. Otto Fox and his students are talking after class. Ahmad says, "I see valentine cards and candy hearts in all the stores. What is Valentine's Day?"

Maria looks surprised. "You don't know about Valentine's Day, Ahmad? On Valentine's Day you send cards and gifts to the people you love. I usually get one or two . . ."

"Hey, Mr. Fox," says George. "I have an idea. Let's have a party for Valentine's Day."

Mr. Fox looks angry. "No, George. In my opinion, Valentine's Day is a ridiculous holiday, and I don't like parties in school."

The students are surprised. Otto Fox never gets angry, and he is always kind. The students leave. They walk out slowly and quietly. Nobody feels like talking. Otto sits alone at his desk. He feels bad, too.

"I was wrong to be angry at the students," he thinks. "It's not their fault. Why do I hate Valentine's Day so much?"

Then he remembers. "The first girl I ever liked. I was thirteen years old. She was my next-door neighbor, Connie. She was fifteen, and she was beautiful. I sent her an expensive, romantic valentine card. On the card, I asked her to go to the Valentine's Day dance with me. I waited and waited for an answer."

Otto Fox shakes his head. "Two days later, I met Connie on the way to school," he remembers. "She smiled at me and said, 'Otto, thanks so much for the beautiful card. That was so sweet. But I can't go to the dance with you because . . .' I ran away. I didn't wait for Connie to finish. I knew then that it was silly for me to ask her. She was fifteen . . . I was only thirteen. I was so embarrassed."

Otto smiles. "It's silly to hate Valentine's Day now, 21 years later," he tells the empty classroom. "I know what I'm going to do! I am going to surprise the students. I am going to give them a party tomorrow. I feel better already."

Otto gets up from his desk and walks down the stairs and out of the school. He is happy. He catches the bus for home. He enters his apartment building and opens his mailbox. Inside it is a large, red envelope. "What's this?" he thinks. He opens the envelope and finds an expensive, romantic valentine. There is no signature—only the words, "Happy Valentine's Day from your secret admirer." Otto smiles and walks upstairs to his apartment.

(To be continued. This is Part 1 of a two-part story.)

What's in the Story?

Answer these questions about "Valentine's Day" (Part 1). Use complete sentences, and write on your own paper. You can find the answers in the story.

1. What is Valentine's Day?
2. What does George want to do on Valentine's Day?
3. Why are the students surprised at Mr. Fox?
4. Who was Connie?

5. What did Otto send to Connie?
6. How old was Otto at the time?
7. What did Connie say to Otto about the card?
8. What did Connie say to Otto about the dance?
9. How old is Otto Fox?
10. What does Otto find in his mailbox?

What Do You Think?

Answer these questions. Use the story and your own ideas. Write on your own paper.

1. Ahmad asks, "What is Valentine's Day?" Why doesn't she know about Valentine's Day?
2. Mr. Fox is angry when Maria talks about Valentine's Day. Why?
3. Connie says, "I can't go to the dance with you because . . ." but Otto doesn't wait for her to finish. Why can't Connie go to the dance with Otto?
4. Why does Otto feel better after he thinks about the past?
5. Otto opens his mailbox and finds a valentine card from a secret admirer. Who can the secret admirer be?

Valentine's Day—Part 2

The next day Otto entered the room carrying a large box. He was smiling and happy. The students were glad to see that Mr. Fox was not still angry.

"I want to apologize for getting angry yesterday," Otto told the class. "I was upset about something that happened on Valentine's Day a long time ago. It was silly. Of course, we don't all have the same opinion about Valentine's Day. It's all right for my opinion and yours to be different." He smiled at the class.

"I want you to enjoy Valentine's Day," Otto said, "so I bought this cake for all of you. We can get coffee and other drinks from the cafeteria. Then we can have a little celebration."

The students gathered around Otto Fox's desk. "Let's get organized," he said. "George, here's five dollars. Can you and Tin-Sek go up to the cafeteria and get the drinks?" Mr. Fox looked around and said, "George, you take the orders. Don't forget cream and sugar for the coffee and tea."

"Now let's put the desks in a circle and make sure everyone gets a napkin," Otto added. "I don't want a mess."

Maria smiled at Juli and said, "Same old Mr. Fox."

"And you, Ahmad," continued Mr. Fox, "cut the cake."

Mr. Fox opened the box. Inside was a beautiful cake. It was shaped like a heart and had pink frosting. Around the edges there were pink and white flowers, and in the center were the words, "Be My Valentine."

"Oh, Mr. Fox! It's beautiful! We can't cut it," said Trang.

Alain laughed. "Don't listen to her. I'm hungry. Cut the cake, Ahmad," he said. Just then George and Tin-Sek came back with the drinks, and everyone sat down to eat and talk.

"Did everyone get a valentine?" asked Mr. Fox.

George laughed. "Well, you know me. I got one from every girl I know."

"Not from me," said Maria, making a face.

"Not from me," said Trang, Juli, and Ahmad, all talking at the same time.

Mr. Fox laughed. "Now tell the truth, George. How many did you really receive?"

"O.K. I admit it. None. But you know how the mail is these days."

"I got one, George," said Alain. "The mail isn't so slow."

"You know," said Ahmad, "I sent a valentine card to my boyfriend back home. I can't wait till he writes me back. I am sure he never saw one before."

"You're single, aren't you, Mr. Fox?" asked George. "Did you get any valentines?"

"Yes, I'm single, and yes, I received a valentine. That's why we're celebrating."

"Excuse me, Mr. Fox, but can you tell us who sent you the valentine?" asked Juli.

"That's a secret," said Mr. Fox, smiling. "Now let's get this mess cleaned up."

What's in the Story?

Answer these questions about "Valentine's Day" (Part 2). Use complete sentences and write on your own paper. You can find the answers in the story.

1. What kind of mood is Otto Fox in on Valentine's Day?
2. How did Mr. Fox surprise the students?
3. What did Mr. Fox ask George and Tin-Sek to do?
4. Describe the cake.
5. Why didn't Trang want to cut the cake?

6. What did the students do at the party?
7. How many valentines did George receive?
8. Is Mr. Fox married?

What Do You Think?

Answer these questions. Use the story and your own ideas. Write on your own paper.

1. Why did Otto change his mind and give the party?
2. Maria says to Juli, "Same old Mr. Fox." What does she mean?
3. What do the girls think of George?
4. Why does Mr. Fox end the party?
5. George asks Mr. Fox if he is single. Do only single people get valentines?

Fact and Opinion

A fact is a statement that most people accept to be true. You can check facts in an encyclopedia, dictionary, or other reference book. You can also prove facts by experiments. Look at the sentence below:

Water freezes at 32°F or 0°C.

This statement is a fact because you can prove it with an experiment or by checking in a science book. Now look at this sentence:

Winter is a terrible season.

Is this a fact? Can you prove it with an experiment? Can you check it in a dictionary or encyclopedia? No. This statement is an opinion. It is a personal feeling. There is nothing scientific or measurable about it. One person may believe that winter is a terrible season. Another may believe that winter is a wonderful season.

Look at the twenty statements below. Decide if each one is a fact or an opinion. If the statement is a fact, write "Fact" on your paper. If it is an opinion, write "Opinion" on your paper. Be ready to tell why you judged each one as you did.

1. There are fifty states in the United States.
2. History is more interesting than science.

3. Whales are mammals.
4. Summer is the best season of the year.
5. There are 52 weeks in a year.
6. Dogs are the best pets.
7. China is a country in Asia.
8. The sun is a star.
9. Light travels at 186,000 miles a second.
10. Blue is the prettiest color.
11. Stamp collecting is fun.
12. English has more than 800,000 words.
13. Nursing is the most exciting medical career.
14. Cake is better than ice cream.
15. Many people around the world are bilingual.
16. Strawberries are delicious.
17. English is the official language of the United States.
18. Cats sleep more than people.
19. Everyone loves Valentine's Day.
20. Alexander Graham Bell invented the telephone.

Facts and Opinions in Advertising

It is important to know the difference between fact and opinion when you read or hear advertisements. Every company wants you to think that its product is the biggest, the best, the most important to your life, or the most exciting. These are opinions. Learn to listen and read for the facts. The facts give you information you can use to make good decisions.

Read the following advertisements. On your paper, write one fact and one opinion found in each advertisement. The first one is done for you.

1. Valentine's Day is February 14. It's the most important day of the year because it's the day you show how much you care. Remember your loved ones with a card from Lyle's Gift Shop. Lyle's has the most beautiful cards in town, and we're open until 9:00 every night.

   Fact: *Valentine's Day is February 14.*

   Opinion: *Lyle's has the most beautiful cards in town.*

2. The teenage years are the best years of your life. Don't let skin problems spoil these years. Many teenagers have problems with their skin. Now there is help: Erasercream! It can make your teenage years beautiful!

3. Tired of waiting for the school bus? Think about a bike! Bikes use *your* energy—they don't need expensive gasoline! A bike is ready when you are—and bikes are cheaper than cars! Everyone enjoys bicycle riding, so what are you waiting for? Get a bike! Mikes's Bikes is open from 9 to 6, Monday through Saturday. Walk in and ride out!

4. Omega Airlines flies from New York to Miami every hour on the hour around the clock. We offer the lowest fares in town, our meals are delicious, and our service is the friendliest in the country! Fly Omega the next time you go to Florida. You'll be glad you did!

5. Phoning long distance costs much less today than it did five years ago. Now most countries have a code that you can dial yourself. This makes your calls fast, simple, and inexpensive. Call today and enjoy a chat with family and friends far away. Calling long distance is the best way to let loved ones know that you care.

6. You can run like the wind in Break-away action shoes! You'll look smart, and your feet will be cool and comfortable! What's more, these action shoes are great for any sport, indoors or out—tennis, jogging, basketball, squash, you name it! Breakaway action shoes are on sale at Burnside Department Stores this week, so come in and break away! Break-away action shoes are made in the United States.

7. Announcing the Grand Opening of Fairview Meadows Shopping Mall, this Monday at 9:30. Come for the fun! See the newest and best shopping mall in the United States! Visit 64 stores under one roof! There are department stores, specialty stores, drug stores, restaurants, and even a video arcade! You are going to love this new mall!

8. *First Sunday in April* is playing this week at the Courtside Theater. Lana Young and Tom Grayson star in the most enjoyable romantic movie of the year. *First Sunday in April*, now playing at the Courtside—you're going to love it!

9. Visit New Hampshire, the most beautiful of the fifty states! We have clear, sparkling lakes, towering mountains, and clean parks for you to visit and enjoy. Our people are warm and friendly, and our stores are open seven days a week. Best of all, there's no state tax on the things you buy. Come up and visit us this summer in lovely New Hampshire. There's a welcome waiting!

10. Woodhole Furniture's annual sale begins tomorrow, March 25. Our doors are open at 9 AM. Come in and see the most beautiful furniture at the best prices! We have the furniture you want at a price you can afford. Coffee and doughnuts are free while you shop.

Who started all this love business? Some people say it was . . .

CUPID

Cupid is the chubby little boy with wings that we see on Valentine's Day cards. He carries a bow and arrow and is a symbol of romance. In ancient Greece and Rome, Cupid (the Greeks called him Eros) was the god of love. He was invisible and flew around shooting people with his arrows. The people he shot fell in love with the first person they met. Sometimes Cupid played cruel jokes on people and made them fall in love with animals or with people they hated.

Once Cupid cut himself with his own arrow by accident and fell in love with a human named Psyche. She became his wife, and after many problems they had a child called Pleasure.

Today, Cupid is still making people happy and sad, breaking hearts and causing problems. Just the same, most of us think that love is worth all the trouble.

Information, Please

Use facts from the reading and your own knowledge and ideas. Write your answers on a separate piece of paper.

1. What does Cupid look like?
2. Is Cupid a real person?
3. What is Cupid a symbol of?
4. What is Cupid's Greek name?
5. What does Cupid do to make people fall in love?
6. What kind of tricks does Cupid play?
7. How did Cupid fall in love?
8. Who was Cupid's wife?

Fact or Opinion?

Read the sentences below. On a separate paper write "Fact" if the statement is a fact. Write "Opinion" if the statement is an opinion.

1. The Greeks and Romans had different names for the god of love.
2. The ancient Romans called their god of love Cupid.
3. The story about Cupid is a beautiful story.
4. Falling in love is worth all the trouble.
5. Today, many people buy Valentine's Day cards with pictures of Cupid.

Predicting Outcomes

According to the story, what happens if a sleeping person, shot with Cupid's arrow, awakes and the first thing he or she sees is a frog? What do you think that person is going to do? Write your answer on a separate piece of paper.

Talking about You

1. Do you celebrate Valentine's Day in your country?
2. Is Valentine's Day your favorite holiday? Why or why not? If it is not, what is your favorite holiday? Why?
3. What holidays or holiday traditions are important in your country? How are they celebrated?

Composition Corner

1. Do you have an embarrassing or unhappy memory from long ago? Tell what happened and how you felt. How do you feel about it now? Write about your ideas in a paragraph or two.
2. Valentine's Day, Christmas, and Thanksgiving are usually happy times. They make some people sad, however. Why do you think some people are sad on these and other holidays? Write about your ideas.

6. WHERE AM I?

Getting lost can be a terrible experience. Read the next story and see what happens when Tin-Sek's mother, who can't speak English, gets lost.

It was six o'clock on a cold, windy evening in March. Outside, the last of the snow was almost gone, but spring was still several weeks away. Inside Tin-Sek's house, in the warm kitchen, the family was busy preparing dinner.

"I wonder where Mother is," said Mae Ling. "She's usually home from work by now."

"I hope she's all right," said Tin-Sek, chopping vegetables.

"Probably the bus was late or she had to work overtime," said Mae Lee. "Don't get upset, Mae Ling. You're always nervous about something!"

"Well, I am upset," Mae Ling answered. "I'm worried." She ran to the window and looked out. The street was empty. "Call Mrs. Lee and see if she's home yet," she told her brother.

Tin-Sek called Mrs. Lee's number. He spoke for a few minutes and hung up.

"What's the matter?" asked Mae Ling. "Now you look upset."

"Mrs. Lee didn't go to work today. Mother went alone and she has to come home alone," answered Tin-Sek.

"Don't look so worried," said Mae Lee. "She's not that late."

"I know something's wrong. This is only her second week on the job and she doesn't speak any English. She can't even ask anyone for help."

"What are we going to do?" asked Mae Ling.

"I'm going out to look for her," said Tin-Sek.

Just then the telephone rang. Tin-Sek ran to answer it. An excited voice said in Chinese, "Tin-Sek? I'm lost. I don't know how to get home."

"Mother!" said Tin-Sek. "Where are you?"

"Well, I took a bus, but it was the wrong bus. I got off, and I walked and walked . . . I don't know where I am."

"Look around. What do you see?"

"It's dark and I can't see anything."

"Look again. Are there stores or houses around?"

"No. There's a big iron gate but it's dark and I can't see what's behind it."

"Can you see anything else?"

"Well, I can't see anything, but it smells funny here."

"Funny?"

"Yes, like a farm."

"But mother, this is the city."

"Oh I hear noises. No . . . it can't be! It sounds like an elephant!"

"Don't you know, mother?" Tin-Sek laughed. "You're at the zoo! Stay where you are. I'm coming!"

Forty-five minutes later the kitchen door opened and Tin-Sek and his mother walked in.

"Oh mother," said Mae Ling. "Thank goodness. We were so worried. Here, come sit down and have dinner. Everything is ready."

Mrs. Tang looked surprised.

The family sat down and began to eat. Mrs. Tang laughed. "You know," she said, "this food is delicious. I don't know why, but food always tastes better when someone else cooks it." She looked at her children and smiled. "Maybe it's a good idea to get lost every once in a while."

What's in the Story?

Answer these questions about "Where Am I?" Use complete sentences and write on your own paper. You can find the answers in the story.

1. Why was Mae Ling worried?
2. What was Tin-Sek doing in the kitchen?
3. Who is Mrs. Lee?
4. When did Tin-Sek's mother begin her job?
5. Does Tin-Sek's mother speak English?
6. Who called Tin-Sek on the telephone?
7. How did Tin-Sek's mother get lost?
8. How did Tin-Sek know that his mother was at the zoo?
9. How long did it take Tin-Sek to find his mother and bring her back home?
10. What does Mrs. Tang say about dinner?

What Do You Think?

Answer these questions. Use the story and your own ideas. Write on your own paper.

1. What kind of son is Tin-Sek?
2. How is Mae Lee different from Mae Ling?
3. Why does Mrs. Tang go to work with Mrs. Lee?
4. Mrs. Lee didn't go to work but Mrs. Tang went alone. What kind of person is Mrs. Tang?
5. Mrs. Tang looks surprised when she sees that dinner is ready. Why?
6. What does Mrs. Tang mean when she says, "It's a good idea to get lost every once in a while."

Following Directions

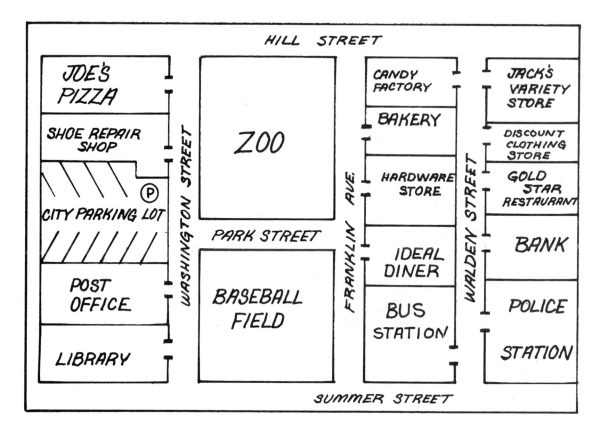

Use the map above to answer the following questions. Write your answers on a separate paper. The first example is answered for you.

1. You're on the corner of Washington and Summer Street. You are across from the library.
   a. Where are you? *I'm at the baseball field.*
   b. What are you going to do? *I'm going to play baseball.*

2. You park your car at the city parking lot. You turn left when you leave the lot. You stop at the second shop you see.
   a. Where are you?
   b. What are you going to do there?

3. You leave the bus station and turn left on Walden Street. You walk up Walden and go into the fourth building on the right.
   a. Where are you?
   b. What are you going to do there?

4. You are on Franklin Avenue in the third building from the corner of Hill Street.
   a. Where are you?
   b. What are you going to do there?

5. You are at the library doing your homework. You remember that tomorrow is your brother's birthday. You want to buy a cake.
   a. Where are you going?
   b. How are you going to get there from the library?

6. You are at the parking lot where you left your car. It isn't there. You are afraid someone stole it.
   a. Where are you going?
   b. How are you going to get there from the lot?

7. You and your friends are eating dinner at the Gold Star Restaurant. You remember that you have to do a report for school.
   a. Where are you going?
   b. How are you going to get there from the restaurant?

8. You are at the bank, taking some money out. You remember that you have to mail a package to your brother back home in your country.
   a. Where are you going?
   b. How are you going to get there from the bank?

Mrs. Tang was missing for only a few hours, but many lost people never come home. Read about these . . .

MISSING PERSONS

Every year the police in the United States receive thousands of reports about missing persons. A missing person is someone who disappears without any explanation. Some of these people stay missing for a few days or weeks. Some remain missing for years. Some disappear and nobody ever sees them again.

No one knows the exact number of adults who vanish every year. The police estimate that the number could be as high as 250,000. Most of these people, say the police, leave home to escape problems and responsibilities. The majority of this group return to their homes after a short period of time, but some stay away forever.

If the missing person chose to leave home, the family cannot expect much practical help from the police. It is not a crime to disappear or run away from home. Even if the police find a missing person, they cannot force him or her to return home. That must be the missing person's own choice.

Of course, some missing persons do not choose to disappear. Police estimate that five to ten percent of all missing adults are victims of accidents or of crime, such as murder or kidnaping.

What can the family of a missing person do? They can try to find out where that person was just before he or she disappeared. They can call the person's friends, workplace, or school. They can talk to neighbors and anyone else who saw the person on the day he or she disappeared. The family should also check the missing person's room to see if clothes or other belongings are missing. If the missing person is a teenager or young adult, the family can call a Missing Persons hotline.

The family should also call the police. The police will ask for a description of the missing person, the date when the person disappeared, and so on. They will use this information to check reports of accident victims. They will try to find out about the missing person in other ways, too.

If you know anything about a missing person, tell the police what you know. If it is someone who ran away, and you don't want to break a promise to that person, try to convince him or her to get in touch with parents or other family members. That way they will know the person is safe. Anything you can do to reduce the pain and heartbreak of the families of missing persons will earn their gratitude forever.

Information, Please

Use facts from the reading and your own knowledge and ideas. Write your answers on a separate piece of paper.

1. What is a missing person?
2. How many adults disappear each year in the United States?
3. Why do some people choose to disappear?
4. What can you do if a friend or someone in your family disappears?

What's the Message?

What is the main idea of this reading? Write your answer on your own paper.

a. It is wrong to run away from home and cause your family pain and worry.

b. Families and police should work together to bring the missing persons home.

c. Every year in the United States, thousands of adults disappear without an explanation, causing great pain to their families.

d. Only five to ten percent of adult missing persons are victims of crime or accidents.

Supporting Details

On your paper, list four other statements that explain or prove the main idea statement you chose.

Giving Directions

A friend who lives near your school is going to visit you this weekend. Draw a map to show your friend how to get from the school to your house or apartment. Give the names of the streets and show any landmarks (buildings or signs you pass on the way) that will help your friend find your home. Be sure your map is clear, so your friend doesn't get lost!

Talking about You

1. Did you ever get lost? Tell what happened.

2. Do you ever travel on a city bus or subway by yourself? Do you remember the first time you did it alone? Where did you go? How did you know how to get there? Were you nervous? Tell what happened and how you felt.

Composition Corner

1. Write a paragraph that explains the directions from school to your house. Be specific. If you take a bus to school, tell

its number or name. Tell what you see along the way, and give the location of any important landmarks.

2. Think of a time when you were waiting for a friend or a member of your family, and that person was late. Did you worry about what happened to that person? Did you think you made a mistake about the meeting place or time? Were you angry? Write a paragraph explaining what you thought about, how you felt, and what happened when the person finally arrived.

7. GEORGE'S VAN

It's nice to have a car, but it's very important that you learn to be a careful driver. Accidents can happen very easily. Read the next story about George and his new van.

George's van was bright and shiny and smelled new. He was driving down the street waving to all his neighbors. At the corner of his street he saw his classmates, Tin-Sek, Juan, and Alain.

George said, "Get in, guys. This is my new van. Take a ride with me."

The boys got into the van and George drove toward town.

"Look," said Juan, "There are the girls from our class." George drove over to the girls.

"Can we give you a ride?" asked Alain.

The girls were not sure. "Who's in that van? Whose van is it?" asked Maria.

George smiled. "It's my van. Come on; get in."

Tin-Sek opened the back door. "Juan and I are back here. Climb in. There's plenty of room."

The girls looked at each other. They weren't sure. Finally Ahmad said, "Come on. Let's just look inside." The girls got into the van and sat on the soft leather seats.

"Come with us for a ride," George said.

"Oh no. We can only stay for a minute. We were at the movies and we have to go home," said Juli.

"Oh, just a little ride," said George. Suddenly the van started to move. Tin-Sek closed the door.

"You stop this van right now, George, and let us out," yelled Maria.

"Come on, once around the block. It's not going to kill you."

Juli and Trang looked at each other nervously. Maria was furious. She sat back in her seat and folded her arms. She didn't look at anyone. Ahmad laughed at the other girls. "Just a short ride," she said. "Let's have some fun."

"Look! There's Otto Fox and the supervisor, Ms. Goodwin, together, on a Saturday!" said George. "What do you think of that?" George pulled over to the curb.

"Hey, Mr. Fox, do you want a ride? This is my new van."

"You remember Ms. Goodwin, don't you?" asked Mr. Fox.

"Of course . . . Hi, Ms. Goodwin," said the students.

"Oh, Ms. Goodwin, please take a ride with us," said Trang.

"Can we all fit?" asked Ms. Goodwin.

"Don't worry. This van can fit everybody comfortably," said George, looking proud.

"Sure, if they're sardines," Maria said under her breath. Mr. Fox and Ms. Goodwin got in the van, and George drove off. He left the city and turned onto the highway. He began to drive faster and faster.

"Slow down, George!" said Mr. Fox. George turned around.

"Don't worry, I'm a good driver."

"George, watch the road!" screamed Maria.

George turned around and looked at the road. All of a sudden a huge truck appeared. It was heading straight for the van. George tried to turn, but it was too late. The van was going to crash into the truck. Everyone screamed as the truck hit the van.

 46 *George's Van*

George woke up. His heart was beating hard. He was sweating, but he was alive and in his own bed. There was no van; there was no truck. It was only a dream.

"What an awful nightmare!" thought George. "I'm never going to drive fast again."

What's in the Story?

Answer these questions about "George's Van." Use complete sentences and write on your own paper. You can find the answers in the story.

1. Who were the first passengers in the van?
2. Who saw the girls first?
3. Where were the girls before they met the boys?
4. Which one of the girls wanted to go for a ride?
5. Who was with Mr. Fox?
6. What hit the van?
7. Why did George wake up?
8. What lesson did George learn from this dream?

What Do You Think?

Answer these questions. Use the story and your own ideas. Write on your own paper.

1. Why didn't the girls want to ride with the boys?
2. Why was Maria furious?
3. Why did Trang want Ms. Goodwin to ride with them?
4. George said, "Come on, once around the block. It's not going to kill you." What did he mean?
5. George said, "Look! There's Otto Fox and the supervisor, Ms. Goodwin, together on a Saturday." What did he mean?
6. Maria said that everyone can fit comfortably in the van "if they're sardines." What did she mean? Why did she say it "under her breath"?
7. Why didn't George slow down when Mr. Fox told him to?
8. Was George afraid when he woke up? How do you know?

Something Is Wrong

Below are descriptions of some dreams. Read each dream and answer the questions about it on a separate paper. Read carefully because some things that happen in dreams don't happen in real life.

1. I was walking towards home. As I walked, my house moved farther and farther away. Finally, I turned around and my house was behind me. I went into the house and there was another family living there. They had no faces. They said I could stay there if I took off my face. I was afraid and began to run. They began to chase me, and I woke up screaming.

   a. What usually happens when you walk towards a house?
   b. What happened when the dreamer walked towards the house?
   c. What was the strangest thing about the people in the house?

2. I was taking a shower. Suddenly the water became very hot, but it didn't burn me. I felt myself shrinking. I became smaller and smaller until I found myself swimming in deep water in the bottom of the bathtub. I tried to climb onto a bar of soap but it was too slippery. Finally I gave up and I went down the drain with the hot soapy water.

   a. What happened when the dreamer took a shower?
   b. How do you think the dreamer felt when he or she woke up?

3. I dreamed I had an important test, but I didn't want to study. I met my friend Lucia on the street. She had a completely different face, but somehow I knew it was Lucia. We went to the library to study. We walked in and saw many tables and chairs. We sat down.
   A man came over to our table and said, "May I help you?" Lucia said, "We'll have two orders of algebra, please." The man brought two plates with books on them. Lucia said, "Let's eat. We have a test tomorrow, you know." Lucia began to eat one of the books. I took a bite of my book and soon I began to feel more confident about the test. "You know, Lucia," I said, "algebra's not so bad after all."

a. What two places does the dreamer mix together in this dream?

b. What is the strangest thing that happens in this story?

c. Do you think the dreamer felt happy or upset after this dream? Why?

4. I dreamed I was flying from New York to Rio de Janeiro, Brazil.

   The flight attendant's voice came over the intercom. "We will arrive in Rio in five minutes. Please take off your seat-belts and prepare to leave the plane." Then the flight attendant opened the door of the plane. There were clouds right outside the door. The passengers made a line, and one by one they jumped out. I looked out the window. Far away, down on the ground, people were catching the passengers.

   a. As the plane approaches Rio, the flight attendant in the dream says, "Take off your seatbelts and prepare to leave the plane." What does a flight attendant usually say?

   b. Why didn't the passengers in the dream need para-chutes?

5. Several soldiers in uniform were chasing me down the street. I ran and ran, but I couldn't get away from them. Suddenly, they began shooting. The bullets hit me, but they didn't hurt me. Then I knew the soldiers had no power over me. I stopped running and waited for them. I punched each one and they all ran away, screaming, "Help! Help!"

   a. How does the dreamer realize that the soldiers are harmless?

   b. Does this dream have a happy or a sad ending? Why?

6. I was babysitting for a three-month-old baby. He was smiling and playing. All of a sudden, he sat up and began talking. He told me to get him some candy and cookies. I knew a three-month-old baby shouldn't have candy or cookies, but I couldn't help myself. I felt I had to obey him.

   a. What does this baby do that is unusual for a three-month-old baby?

   b. Why do you think the dreamer obeyed the baby?

   c. What do you think the baby in the dream asked for next?

STOP

7. I was a passenger on a ship. We were on a cruise in the Caribbean Sea. One minute we were all sunbathing and enjoying ourselves. The next minute, there was a big crash and people began to scream. The ship had hit an iceberg and we were sinking. I felt that I could save the ship. I jumped into the water and swam under the ship. Somehow, I lifted the sinking ship and held it up until everyone got off the ship safely and into the lifeboats.

   a. Why is it strange that the ship in this dream hit an iceberg?
   b. How did the dreamer save the passengers on the ship?

8. I was in the hospital. The doctors and nurses all wore black uniforms. A nurse brought me some pills. I told the nurse I felt fine and that I wanted to go home. He said, "Of course you feel fine. We want you to feel fine. Tomorrow the doctors are going to remove your heart and liver. Someone else needs them." I began to struggle and fight, but the nurse tied me to the bed.

   a. What makes the doctors and nurses appear evil in this dream?
   b. How is the operation planned in this dream unusual?
   c. How do you think the dreamer felt when he or she woke up?

*Don't take a chance with your life
while driving . . .*

BE CAREFUL!

More than 120 million motor vehicles (cars, buses, trucks, and motorcycles) travel on U.S. highways. Most of the people who drive these vehicles are responsible and careful. However, some drivers are reckless, and dangerous to themselves and others. Each year in the United States, 50,000 people die in car accidents. Eight thousand of these are teen-agers. Car accidents injure almost two million people every year. Some injuries are only minor cuts and bruises, but others are very serious. Some accidents result in the loss of an arm or a leg. Others result in paralysis.

Accidents are expensive, too. Insurance companies pay eight and a half billion dollars to their customers each year because of accidents. This money pays for car repair and medical bills. Car repairs are very expensive. Hospital bills are even more costly. Many times, insurance doesn't pay the whole bill. Then an accident can be very expensive for an individual as well as the insurance company.

Why are there so many accidents? Unfortunately, it is because there are too many people on the roads who don't take driving seriously. They drive after drinking, or they drive too fast, or they drive without paying attention to traffic signals or other cars. Ninety percent of accidents happen because drivers are being careless. Only ten percent of accidents happen because of bad road conditions or car problems.

If you want to be a good driver, follow these rules:

1) Never drive after drinking alcohol.
2) Always wear your seatbelt.
3) Don't drive too fast for the road you are traveling on.
4) Stay in your lane. Do not pass on hills or at curves.
5) Be alert at intersections.
6) Don't hurry. Give yourself enough time to get where you're going.
7) Always signal if you are going to turn or change lanes.
8) Don't drive when you are angry or upset.

These safety rules aren't very difficult, but they are important. Remember them when you're behind the wheel. Be a responsible motorist, drive safely, and live.

Information, Please

Use facts from the reading and your own knowledge and ideas. Write your answers on a separate piece of paper.

1. How many people die in car accidents in the United States each year?
2. When can an accident be expensive for an individual?
3. Why are there so many traffic accidents?
4. According to the safety rules, when is it dangerous to drive?
5. When is it important for a driver to wear a seatbelt?

Predicting Outcomes

What can happen if you don't follow the safety rules? Answer the questions below on a separate piece of paper.

1. Why is it important to wear a seatbelt when you're driving?

2. Imagine you are driving up a long hill on a two-lane street and you are behind a very slow truck. What can happen if you pull into the other lane and try to pass the truck?

3. What can happen if you forget to signal before you slow down to make a left-hand turn?

Something Is Wrong

Each statement below is false. Change one word or phrase in each sentence to make it true. Rewrite the sentences on your own paper.

1. More than 120 billion vehicles travel on U.S. highways and roads.

2. Paralysis is a minor injury.

3. Insurance companies pay over eight and a half billion dollars to their employees.

4. Ninety per cent of all traffic accidents are caused by bad road conditions.

5. It is difficult to follow the safety rules for good driving.

Talking About You

1. Do you drive? Are you a careful driver? If you don't drive yet, do you want to learn? Why or why not? What do you have to do to get a driver's license?

2. Is there any difference in the way people drive in the United States and in your country?

3. What do you dream about? Do you remember your dreams? Do you ever dream in English?

Composition Corner

1. A daydream is a fantasy you have when you are awake. It helps you to pass the time if you are bored or inactive. A daydream can be happy plans for your future, or a wonder-

ful fantasy in which your hopes, dreams, ambitions, or desires come true. Write a paragraph about a daydream of yours.

2. A nightmare is a scary dream. Have you ever had a nightmare? Is there a nightmare that you have had several times? Write a paragraph describing what happened in your nightmare. Write about how you felt when you woke up.

STOP

8. THE PROMISE

The students in Mr. Fox's class are having a discussion. Read the next story and find out how Alain came to the United States.

"Actually I am here because of a promise," said Alain. "When I was born my aunt and uncle became my godparents. They promised to take care of me if anything happened to my parents.

"I had a happy childhood and spent school vacations with my godparents and their children. We were very close and my cousins thought of me as their little brother. I saw my first movie with them and took my first airplane ride when I went to visit them. On Sunday afternoons, my uncle and I went to soccer matches together. I loved those summers. When I was nine my godparents moved to the U.S. I was sad at first, but we kept in touch through letters."

"Continue, Alain," said Mr. Fox, "you're doing quite well."

"Don't stop now, Alain, this is a good story," said George.

"Well, I am afraid the next part isn't so good. The summer when I was fourteen my parents left for France to attend my cousin's wedding. I stayed home with my grandmother. The day after they left we received a telegram. My parents were dead. Their plane crashed at Orly airport. There were no survivors."

The class sat quietly.

"Oh how awful, Alain," said Juli. There were tears in her eyes.

"Yes," said Alain, "it was a terrible experience. But even worse, my grandmother had a stroke when she heard the news."

"Oh, Alain," said Mr. Fox, "you poor kid."

Alain looked at the students. They all looked sad and sympathetic. Alain smiled.

"Don't feel bad, it was a while ago. I'm fine now. Of course, some days I do still feel bad."

"Who took care of you?" asked Trang.

"Well, at first I stayed with some cousins. Then my grandmother got out of the hospital and she and I lived together. But before that, my aunt and uncle came back for the funeral. It was then that I learned about the promise. My aunt and uncle were going to take me to live with them in the U.S. My grandmother was going to come and live with us too. It took my uncle more than a year to arrange everything legally. At last I arrived in the U.S. Of course I miss my parents and my country, but my new family and my new home are wonderful."

The class began to applaud. Mr. Fox got up and shook Alain's hand. "Well done. Thank you for sharing your story with us."

"And I forgot to say one thing," Alain added. "My new friends are wonderful too."

Everyone smiled.

What's in the Story?

Answer these questions about "The Promise." Use complete sentences and write on your own paper. You can find the answers in the story.

1. Who is telling the story?
2. Who made the promise?
3. What did Alain do on his summer vacations when he was young?
4. Why did Alain's parents go to France?
5. How did Alain's parents die?
6. What happened to Alain's grandmother?
7. When did Alain learn about "the promise"?
8. How long did it take for Alain to come to the U.S.?
9. How does Alain feel about his new home?
10. What did the class do after Alain told his story?

What Do You Think?

Answer these questions. Use the story and your own ideas. Write on your own paper.

1. Alain says, "Actually I am here because of a promise." This is the answer to a question. What was the question?
2. After Alain said his parents were killed, the class was silent. Why?
3. Why were there tears in Juli's eyes?
4. What does "poor" mean in "Oh you poor kid"?
5. What kind of people are Alain's godparents?

Cause and Effect

A *cause* is an action or event that makes something else happen. You learned in the last chapter that drunken driving is the cause of many car accidents. An *effect* is the result or outcome of a particular event. One effect of a serious car accident can be the driver's death.

Look at the six pictures. Tell what caused each action to happen. Then tell what effect each action has.

 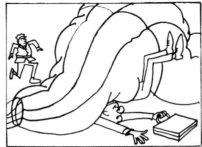 

What's the Effect?

Read the paragraphs carefully, then choose the best answer. Write the answers on your own paper.

1. Alain's parents died in a plane crash. One effect of this is:

    a. Alain's aunt and uncle made a promise.
    b. Alain spent the summer with his godparents.
    c. Alain came to America.
    d. Alain's cousins were nice to him.

2. To pasteurize milk, manufacturers heat it to 161°F. and keep it at that temperature for 15 seconds. Before people knew how to pasteurize milk, many people got sick or died from the bacteria in milk. The effect of pasteurization on milk is:

    a. It freezes the milk.
    b. It kills the bacteria in milk.
    c. It turns the milk sour.
    d. People used to drink unpasteurized milk.

3. During the 1970's there was a gasoline crisis in the United States. Gasoline became expensive and there wasn't always enough for everyone. American cars were large; they used lots of gasoline. Many people didn't want to spend so much money on gasoline or use up so much gasoline. People in the United States began to buy small foreign cars. American companies lost a lot of business. One effect of the gasoline crisis on American car companies was:

    a. The price of gasoline came down.
    b. Gasoline became hard to buy.
    c. Foreign cars broke down easily.
    d. They began to make smaller cars, too.

4. In the 1970's many American businesses began to move. They left the northern states and moved to the Sunbelt, the states in the southern and southwestern part of the United States. As industries moved, working people began to move too. The 1980 U.S. census, a survey of the number of people in the country and where they live, showed that one effect of business relocation was:

    a. higher population in the Northeast
    b. higher unemployment in the South
    c. higher population in the Sunbelt
    d. lower population in the Southwest

5. A famine is a time when there is little or no food for people to eat. Sometimes there is a famine because there isn't enough rain and the crops don't grow. Other times, war causes famine. Whatever the reason, a famine has one certain effect. Which of the following is it?

    a. no water
    b. hunger
    c. bad weather
    d. heat

6. When the Earth rotates, it turns on its axis. The Earth rotates once every 24 hours. One side of the Earth faces the sun for 12 hours while the other part faces away from the sun for the same amount of time. The Earth never stops rotating. Which of the following is an effect of the Earth's rotation?

    a. the four seasons
    b. thunder and lightning
    c. hurricanes and tornadoes
    d. night and day

7. Every day factories pour thousands of tons of smoke and chemicals into our air and water. An effect of this is:

    a. unemployment
    b. bigger factories
    c. new chemicals
    d. pollution

8. A solar eclipse occurs when the moon passes directly between the sun and the Earth. The moon blocks the rays of the sun from hitting the Earth. The effect of the eclipse is:

    a. darkness on the Earth
    b. movement of the sun
    c. a longer day
    d. darkness on the moon

9. It is important to prepare the wood before you paint a house. First you must wash the wood, then you must remove any loose paint. The new paint will not remain on the wood for long if you do not prepare the surface well. The effect of painting over dirty wood or loose paint is:

   a. the new paint will last longer
   b. the new paint will come off
   c. you must wash the wood
   d. the house looks better

10. Many people plant shade trees near their houses. These trees keep the rays of the sun off the house in the summer, but allow the sun to shine on the house in the winter, when the leaves are off the trees. One effect of planting shade trees near your house is:

   a. planting trees in the summer
   b. a cooler house in the summer
   c. lower house prices
   d. shorter winters and longer summers

When Alain finished his story he heard . . . .

APPLAUSE

In many parts of the world people clap hands to show that they like or approve of something. In the theater, at a concert, or at a football game, people clap hands after they see something they like. In Russia the actors, performers, and athletes clap with the audience. In most countries, however, the performers are happy to receive the applause. They don't clap back to their fans.

A very long time ago clapping meant the opposite of what it means now. When people did not like an actor or a performer they clapped. They were trying to make as much noise as possible. They continued to clap until the actor left the stage.

At some time in history the meaning of clapping changed. It became a compliment instead of an insult. Now when an audience wants to show great admiration for a performer, they not only clap but they stand up and clap. That is called a standing ovation. A standing ovation is the dream of every performer. Many actors say that is what they work so hard for—Applause! Applause!

Information, Please

Use facts from the reading and your own knowledge and ideas. Write your answers on a separate piece of paper.

1. Why do people clap their hands?
2. In what situations do people clap their hands?
3. What do Russian performers do after a show?
4. Why did people clap in the old days?
5. What is a standing ovation?

What's the Effect?

Read the paragraph carefully, then write the best answer.

Many times at a night club or concert, the audience applauds for a long time after a singer has finished the show. What is the effect of the applause?

a. The audience enjoyed the show.
b. The ushers make the audience leave the show.
c. People buy more tickets to see the performer.
d. The singer returns to thank the audience and sing another song.

Something Is Strange

One word in each sentence below makes that statement strange and untrue. On your own paper, rewrite each sentence using a different word to make the statement true.

1. When people enjoy a show very much, they stand up and wave their hands.

2. Most performers feel insulted when they hear applause.

3. A standing ovation is every performer's nightmare.

Talking About You

1. Many people are afraid to speak in front of a group. Are you? Why or why not?

2. Have you ever performed before a group of people? What did you do? Did people applaud you? How did you feel?

3. Do you dream about becoming a star—an actor, a musician, a singer or a dancer? Would you like to perform before thousands of people some day? Why or why not?

4. Tell your story about coming to the United States. Why did you or your family decide to come? When did you come? How did you get here?

Composition Corner

1. Did anyone ever make you a promise? Did they keep their promise? If not, why not? Write about the promise. Tell what happened and how you felt. Tell why you think it is important to keep a promise.

2. Do you have a favorite aunt, uncle, or cousin? Write about that person and tell what makes him or her special. Include in your composition the things you do together.

3. Write about a sad experience you had in the past. How did you feel then? How do you feel now?

9. THE MISSING TICKETS

The tickets to the play are missing! No one knows who took them. Read the next story and find out how Juan solves the mystery.

"I feel so excited, Trang," said Juli as they walked up the steps to the classroom on a sunny day in April. "Just think. My first play in English. I hope it's not too difficult to understand. Good morning, Mrs. Braverman."

"Good morning, Juli." Mrs. Braverman, the school principal, was standing outside their classroom. "Did you see Mr. Fox this morning? I have the transportation passes to the play for your class."

"No, Mrs. Braverman. We just arrived."

Trang smiled. "I'll be happy to look for Mr. Fox."

"No, thank you, Trang. It is almost time for class. You girls finish your conversation. I can return later."

As Mrs. Braverman walked away, Tin-Sek and George came running up the stairs.

"Hi Trang, hi Juli!" cried George. "Is it time to go yet?"

"No, George," laughed Trang. "We have plenty of time." Just then the students heard Mr. Fox's voice.

"Here he comes," shouted George.

"Really, George," said Maria, sticking her head out the class-room door. "Can you lower your voice?"

"Oh Maria, you're no fun. Aren't you excited about the play?"

"Of course, I am. But I don't need to yell my head off just because I'm going to a play."

George opened his mouth to answer. Just then Mr. Fox reached the top of the stairs. He looked at Maria and George. "Are you two fighting again?" He didn't wait for them to answer. "Just calm down. We want to have a pleasant day." He walked into the room and the students followed behind.

"Excuse me, Mr. Fox," said Trang, "but Mrs. Braverman was looking for you. She has some bus passes for us. She's coming back in a few minutes."

"Oh, thank you, Trang. That will save me time. I was planning to look for her. All right now," continued Mr. Fox. "Let's get organized. As you know, the play we are going to see is a mystery. The name of the play is *Holmes Sweet Holmes* and it is about the most famous fictional English detective of all time, Sherlock Holmes."

"What does fictional mean?" asked Alain.

"A fictional character, Alain," said Mr. Fox, "is a character who never really lived. The author created him from his own imagination."

Just then there was a knock on the door. Mrs. Braverman walked in carrying an envelope. "Good morning, Mr. Fox," she said.

"Good morning, Mrs. Braverman. I see you have my bus passes."

"Yes, here you are." She turned to the students. "I hope that you all enjoy the play."

After the students thanked Mrs. Braverman and she left, Mr. Fox continued. "Now I am going to give each of you your bus pass and theater ticket. In that way, if you get lost, you can meet us at the door of the theater. Now just let me get the tickets." He unlocked the top drawer of the desk and looked in. He began to move the papers around faster and faster, and then he began to take things out of the drawer and put them on the desk.

"Oh, no," whispered Maria to Trang. "He can't find the tickets."

Mr. Fox looked up. "I want you to know, Maria, that I have an excellent sense of hearing." Maria blushed.

He continued to search, opening one drawer after another. Then he opened his briefcase and emptied it. Nothing. He searched the pockets in his jacket and pants, but the tickets were not there.

He looked up at the students and saw their worried faces. George was the only one who spoke. "Does this mean we can't go, Mr. Fox?"

"No, it doesn't, George. It means we have to find the tickets. I was sure they were in the drawer."

"I bet someone stole them," said Maria. "There are thieves in this school. Last week someone stole $2.00 out of my locker, and one of my friends said someone stole her scarf yesterday."

"This is more serious than $2.00 or a scarf, Maria," said Mr. Fox. "Those tickets cost $5.00 each."

"We have to find the thieves," said George. "My uncle is a policeman. He taught me some things about crime."

"Slow down, let's think about this carefully," said Juan. "Maybe we *can* find the thief. The tickets were here yesterday. So we know that the thief stole them last night or this morning."

"But what kind of person steals nine theater tickets?" asked Trang.

"A teacher, a student, a librarian. Anyone in this school," said Alain. "Anyone in this room," he added.

The students looked at each other.

"Hey," said George, "don't look at me. I'm no thief! I don't believe anyone else here is one, either."

"Of course, nobody here did it," said Mr. Fox. "Why, we aren't sure that someone stole them at all. Maybe I just misplaced them."

Juan was standing by the window thinking. "Mr. Fox, I think the smartest thing to do is to think about what you did before you came into the room."

"That's a good idea, Juan. I came to school by bus. I stopped to pick up my mail at the office, then I went up to the teachers' room."

"What did you do there?" asked Juan.

"Well, I had a cup of coffee and I was telling Ms. Goodwin, the supervisor, about the play and I showed her..." Mr. Fox slapped his forehead. "Oh that's right, I showed her the tickets. I probably left them in the teachers' room."

Without another word, Mr. Fox ran out of the room. Five minutes later he was back. He waved the tickets in the air. "OK, class. Let's go!" He looked at Juan and smiled. "You too, Sherlock," he said.

What's in the Story?

Answer these questions about "The Missing Tickets." Use complete sentences and write on your own paper. You can find the answers in the story.

1. Why did Juli feel excited?
2. Who is Mrs. Braverman?
3. Why was Mrs. Braverman looking for Mr. Fox?
4. Why were George and Maria fighting?
5. What is the name of the play?
6. What is a fictional character?
7. Where did Mr. Fox first look for the tickets? Where else did he look for them?
8. How much did the tickets for the class cost all together?
9. What happened to Maria last week?
10. Where were the tickets?

What Do You Think?

Answer these questions. Use the story and your own ideas. Write on your own paper.

1. Maria says to George, "I don't need to yell my head off." What does it mean when someone yells his or her head off?

2. Maria and George are fighting. Are they serious about their fights? Why do you think so? How do Maria and George feel about each other?

3. What did Mr. Fox really mean when he said, "I want you to know, Maria, that I have an excellent sense of hearing"?

4. Why did Maria blush?

5. Why didn't Mr. Fox think of the solution to the mystery by himself?

6. Mr. Fox slapped his forehead. Why did he do this? (What does this action mean?)

7. Why does Mr. Fox call Juan "Sherlock"?

Drawing Conclusions

When you draw a conclusion, you make a decision about a reading or a situation from the facts and information available. For example, if you walk into a classroom and see several pictures of flowers on the walls of the room, you can draw the conclusion that the teacher in that room likes flowers. You don't have to know the teacher; you are making a decision based on the information you see in the room. In the same way, when you are reading, you receive information that you can use to help you draw a conclusion.

In the story, Mr. Fox is the teacher but he can't solve the mystery of the missing tickets. After you read the story and think about the facts, you can draw a conclusion that he was probably too nervous to think clearly. The story doesn't tell you this directly but you can figure it out from the information the story makes available to you. Of course, you can't be 100% sure that your conclusion is correct. For this reason, it is good to use words like, "probably," "possibly," and "maybe" when you draw a conclusion.

Read each description. Talk about the clues that help you answer the questions.

1. A man is ringing the doorbell of a house. He is holding a heart-shaped box of candy, hiding it behind his back. *What holiday is it?*

2. There is a cabin in the woods. The door and windows are open. There is snow on the ground. There are paw prints leading up to the door and windows. *What was in the cabin*

3. The mailbox in front of the Johnsons' house is filled with letters and advertisements. Newspapers from several days

are outside the door. There is no car in the garage. *Where are the Johnsons?*

4. A table for two in a restaurant has empty dessert plates and coffee cups on it. On a small tray is a $20 tip. *Did the waitress do a good job?*

5. Just beyond an intersection, a police officer has stopped a driver. You can just see the back of a stop sign on the other side of the intersection. *Why did the police officer stop the driver?*

6. A woman is standing outside the gate in an airport. A plane has just landed, and the passengers will soon come out through the gate. The woman looks very happy. *Why is she happy?*

7. There is water six feet deep in the main streets of a small town. People are on the roofs of houses. Others are waving out of second-story windows. *What happened in the town yesterday?*

8. There is a chalk outline of a person on the floor of the living room. Lamps and tables are overturned. *What happened in this room?*

Are You a Good Detective?

Detectives draw conclusions from the clues they find. It is the detective's job to learn as much as possible about:

the crime – what happened.

the victim – the person whom the crime happened to.

the suspects – the people who possibly committed the crime.

the criminal – the person who actually did commit the crime.

the weapon – the object used to commit the crime: gun, knife, poison, etc.

the scene – the place where the crime happened.

the evidence – clues that give information about the crime: fingerprints, bloodstains, etc.

Read the following mysteries. Consider the evidence, then draw a conclusion. Write your answers on your own paper.

1.   "Thanks for calling us, Ma'am," said Detective De Luci. "Some people don't like to talk to the police."

"But it was so terrible, Detective. Those awful screams and then the gunshot. I looked out the window and I could see a tall man running down the street."

"How did you see him, Ma'am? The street lights aren't working in this area."

"Oh, I saw him," the woman said. "You see, there was a full moon."

When was the murder committed?

2.   Detective Crump looked at the scene of the murder. "Very interesting," she said as she picked up a piece of chalk from the floor. "This probably fell out of someone's pocket. What did the victim do for a living?" she asked her assistant.

"Oh, he was an auto mechanic," answered Sergeant Lawrence.

"Well, I think we can begin looking for some suspects," Detective Crump smiled. "At least we have a clue to help us know where to begin."

What is the clue and what kind of person does it point to?

3.   "Well, Captain, what do you think?"

"I don't know, Joe. We'll have to wait for a complete investigation, but I have a feeling that we have a crime on our hands."

"Did anyone smell gasoline before it started?"

"Yes, one of the neighbors thinks she did."

What crime are Joe and the Captain discussing?

4.   "Tell me again what happened, Mrs. Loomis."

"Oh, not again, Detective Harris. I can't."

"Please, Mrs. Loomis."

"All right, if it's necessary. We finished our dinner and I served coffee to the guests. Mr. Smyth took a sip of his coffee. He put down his cup, held his stomach, cried out and fell to the floor, dead."

"Did you hand the cup directly to Mr. Smyth, or did another guest pass it to him?" asked the detective.

What piece of evidence will Detective Harris want to examine? Why?

5.   "Unfortunately, this is a perfect place for a murder, Mr. Thompson."

"Why do you say that, Captain Perez?"

"Well, in the winter almost no one is around. The waves slapping against the rocks can hide the noise of a gunshot, and as for the victim's body . . . Well, it's easy to get rid of it here."

Where does Captain Perez think the murder took place?

6.   The noon whistle blew. Bobby Fernandez was hungry. He was the first one to leave the factory. He ran quickly across the street to the sub shop. It took two minutes for him to get a large ham and cheese sub. As he crossed the street, hurrying back to the factory, a car appeared from nowhere. Bobby didn't have a chance. The car hit him and then sped off. The police are making an official report about this hit-and-run accident.

As close as you can figure, what was the exact time of the crime?

7.   Detective Warren Chan looked around the room. He saw a diamond bracelet on the dresser and a purse stuffed with money on the floor; a mink coat was visible in the open closet. Detective Chan thought to himself, "This wasn't the action of any thief. Whoever was here tonight was here for one reason only—to kill Mrs. Dorothea Pennington."

Why is Detective Chan sure that a thief didn't kill Mrs. Pennington?

8.   "This is one of the most bizarre cases of murder in the history of this village," said Sergeant Meyers.

Detective Valdez agreed, as he explained the strange circumstances of the old woman's death. "Everyone in the village knew Sarah Hopkins was afraid of rodents. And, of course, many people disliked Sarah. We don't really know if somebody planned to kill Sarah, or if this was just a cruel trick intended to scare and punish the old woman. In any case, someone shoved Sarah into her own closet, let loose half a dozen rats, and then locked the closet door. Sarah was trapped, with rats running around her feet and climbing up the walls. No wonder she died."

How do you think Sarah Hopkins died?

*If you liked the mystery of the missing
tickets you're going to love . . . .*

SHERLOCK HOLMES

In 1885 a young doctor named Arthur Conan Doyle opened offices in London. He wanted to be a successful doctor but for some reason he never found enough patients. To pass the time he began to write stories and send them to the newspaper.

Conan Doyle's stories were about a clever detective, Sherlock Holmes. Conan Doyle wrote that Sherlock Holmes lived at 221b Baker Street in London, and people with problems came to him for help. Often police detectives came to Sherlock Holmes with their problems, too. He was able to solve mysteries that the smartest policemen in England were unable to figure out.

Sometimes Sherlock Holmes could solve a mystery without leaving his chair. He listened carefully to the information his clients gave and then figured out the answer. At other times he spent days or weeks looking for clues. Sherlock Holmes traveled to different cities and countries to solve the mysteries. Sometimes he wore disguises and pretended to be an old man, or a sailor. Holmes did anything to find the answer to the mysteries he was working on. His friend Dr. Watson accompanied him on most of his adventures.

Sherlock Holmes is the most famous detective in English literature, but many people don't understand that he is a fictional character, not a real person. The English post offices report that people send mail to Sherlock Holmes at 221b Baker St. every day. He gets more than 2,000 letters every year.

Information, Please

Use facts from the reading and your own knowledge and ideas. Write your answers on a separate piece of paper.

1. What did Arthur Conan Doyle want to be?
2. What is Arthur Conan Doyle famous for?
3. Who bought and read Doyle's stories in 1885?
4. In Doyle's stories, who came to see Sherlock Holmes?

5. In the stories, how do you think the English policemen felt about Sherlock Holmes?

6. How did Sherlock Holmes solve the mysteries?

Drawing Conclusions

Use information given in the reading to draw your own conclusions. Write your answer on a separate piece of paper.

1. Who do you think writes to Sherlock Holmes? Why do they write?

2. Do you think Arthur Conan Doyle answers Sherlock Holmes' mail? Why or why not?

3. You can draw the conclusion from this reading that:
   a. Arthur Conan Doyle was the real Dr. Watson.
   b. Arthur Conan Doyle was more successful as a writer than as a doctor.
   c. Sherlock Holmes answers a lot of mail each year.
   d. London is a city of many mysteries.

Sequence

These sentences are out of order. When they are put in the right sequence, they will tell a story. Read the sentences. Decide which sentence comes first, second, third, etc. On your paper, rewrite the sentences in the correct sequence.

- The people of London loved the mysteries and asked the newspaper to print more.

- Arthur Conan Doyle started writing mystery stories in 1885.

- Today people still read and love the mystery cases solved by the brilliant Sherlock Holmes.

- He named this detective Sherlock Holmes.

- He wrote about a strange fictional character, a brilliant detective who smoked a pipe and played the violin.

- The first Sherlock Holmes mystery stories were printed in a London newspaper.

- Conan Doyle's stories were translated into many languages, and Sherlock Holmes became famous all over the world.

Talking About You

1. Have you ever lost or misplaced something important? Did you find it again? What happened?

2. Did anyone ever accuse you of something you didn't do? How did you feel? What did you do about it?

3. Would you like to become a detective? Why or why not?

Composition Corner

1. Look back at the story of "The Missing Tickets." Write a summary of what happened. Use the correct sequence (what happened first, next, etc.). Don't copy the story. Write the summary in your own words.

2. Write a little mystery story of your own. Your story should include a crime, a victim, a detective, and some clues. Tell how the mystery is solved. Who did it? Why did they do it? What weapon did they use?

10. PLENTY MORE FISH IN THE SEA

Some people are very friendly and just love to talk. The girls meet a very talkative, friendly, and interesting woman in this next story.

"Oh, Maria, it's nice to see you outside of school," said Ahmad, sitting down at the table. "I wanted to talk to you about something."

Maria saw the sad look on Ahmad's face and asked, "What's wrong, Ahmad. Tell me."

"Do you remember the valentine card?"

"Sure, the one you sent to your boyfriend back home."

"Well I just got a letter back from him . . ." The girls saw a middle-aged waitress coming toward their table. They stopped talking.

"What can I get you two young ladies?" she asked, smiling.

"Just coffee for me, please."

"Yes, the same for me, please."

"Coming right up," said the waitress.

"Now tell me what happened, Ahmad," Maria said. "You got the letter from your boyfriend . . ."

"And it was just awful," continued Ahmad. "You see, when I left my country he promised to wait until I finished school and could get married. We loved each other so much. Our parents were friends and wanted us to get married some day."

"So what happened?"

"He met another girl. And they are going to get married. In the letter he said he didn't want to hurt me but . . ."

"Oh, Ahmad, don't cry," said Maria sympathetically.

"That's right. Don't cry, honey. There are plenty more fish in the sea," said the waitress, putting down the coffee.

The girls looked up in surprise. "I heard the whole story," said the waitress as she sat down at the table. Ahmad and Maria looked at each other. What could they do?

The waitress patted Ahmad's hand, "I know just how you feel, dear," she continued. "When I was 16 . . . How old are you, honey?" Ahmad opened her mouth to answer but the woman did not wait to hear. "Just like you, I had a boyfriend. He was handsome and a wonderful dancer. We went out every Saturday night to the Wonderland Ballroom."

"What's the Wonderland Ballroom?" asked Ahmad.

The waitress didn't answer but went on with her story. "In the summer my cousin came to visit. She was very quiet and shy. I brought her to the Wonderland Ballroom one Saturday night. Well, nobody danced with her and I said to Phil—that was my boyfriend—'Phil, dance with her. She's lonely.' Can you guess what happened next?"

"What?" asked Maria and Ahmad.

"Two months later they were engaged."

All three were silent for a moment. Then the woman continued, "I was mad, sad, hurt, upset, and angry. I wanted to kill both of them. But I never let them know."

"Really?" said Ahmad, looking surprised. "You never said anything?"

"Not a word," said the waitress. "I even went to the wedding. And I'm glad I did. Guess who I met there."

 74 *Plenty More Fish in the Sea*

"Who?" asked the girls.

"My future husband, Charlie. Not a very good dancer, but a wonderful man in every other way. Our 30th anniversary is next month. So, you see, it's not so bad. You're young. You can meet somebody else... Why aren't you drinking your coffee?" The waitress got up from the table. "Well, I have to get back to work. Now remember what I told you, honey. Don't cry. By the way," she added, "my name is Millie. Come back sometime and tell me how you're doing." The waitress walked away.

"What a strange woman," said Maria in a whisper. "I can't believe what she did."

"Yes," said Ahmad, "she was strange. But you know, I feel better. Let's finish our coffee."

"OK," said Maria. "But I hope you like it cold."

What's in the Story?

Answer these questions about "Plenty More Fish in the Sea." Use complete sentences and write on your own paper. You can find the answers in the story.

1. Where are Ahmad and Maria meeting?
2. What did Ahmad send to her boyfriend?
3. What did the young people order in the restaurant?
4. Why is Ahmad upset?
5. Where did the waitress and her boyfriend go every Saturday night?
6. What did the waitress like about Phil?
7. When did Millie's cousin come to visit?
8. Why did Phil dance with Millie's cousin?
9. How did Millie feel when Phil and her cousin became engaged?
10. Whom did Millie meet at the wedding?

What Do You Think?

Use the story and your own ideas to answer these questions. Write on your own paper.

1. What do you think Ahmad wrote in the valentine?
2. Why did the girls stop talking when the waitress came to take their order?
3. How old do you think Millie is?
4. The waitress says, "There are plenty more fish in the sea." What does she mean?

5. What is the Wonderland Ballroom?
6. What kind of person is the waitress?
7. Why did Maria say that the waitress is strange?
8. Why did Ahmad feel better after talking to Millie?

Understanding Proverbs

A proverb is a short, well-known saying which contains popular wisdom or advice. People often use proverbs in conversation. For example, Millie tells Ahmad, "There are plenty more fish in the sea." Most native speakers of English know that Millie isn't talking about fish at all. They understand the symbolic meaning of Millie's words, that there are many other boys for Ahmad to meet. Some proverbs will be easy for you to understand. Other will be more difficult.

Below are ten proverbs and explanations of what they mean. For each example, choose the situation in which you could best use that proverb. Write the answer on your paper.

1. Millie says, "There are plenty more fish in the sea." She means that there are many other boys or men that Ahmad will meet and date. In which of the following situations could you use this proverb?

   a. Your brother loses some money.
   b. Someone catches a fish in the ocean.
   c. Your friend asks a girl to the prom, and she says "no."
   d. Your mother burns the fish your family was going to eat.

2. "Necessity is the mother of invention." This proverb means that a difficult situation often forces you to be creative and think of new ways to solve a problem. In which of the following situations could you use this proverb?

   a. A scientist invents a new invention after years of hard work.
   b. An executive forgets her raincoat and uses a plastic bag to cover herself and protect her new suit from the rain.
   c. A woman is going to have a baby.
   d. A student uses an encyclopedia to do a research paper or a report.

3. "The squeaky wheel gets the grease." This proverb means that a person who complains loudly often gets more attention than someone who never complains. In which of the following situations could you use this proverb?

   a. One person in class is always asking for extra help during class time.
   b. A man takes his car to the mechanic whenever it begins to squeak.
   c. Three or four people in a restaurant are laughing and talking loudly.
   d. The teacher finds out that everyone in the room is cheating.

4. "The grass is always greener on the other side of the fence." This proverb means that other people's possessions or situations often seem better than our own. In which situation could you use this proverb?

   a. The family next door has just bought a new lawnmower.
   b. A young teenager thinks that adults have no problems.
   c. Your neighbors are always watering their yard.
   d. Your friend says she likes her car better than yours.

5. "Don't judge a book by its cover." This proverb means that the way something (or somebody) looks on the surface can be very different from the way it really is. In which situation could you use this proverb?

   a. A librarian is putting books on a shelf.
   b. A woman buys a new cover for her sofa.
   c. A good-looking person commits a horrible crime.
   d. A judge makes a wrong decision.

6. "One man's meat is another man's poison." This proverb means that what one person loves, another person may hate. In which situation could you use this proverb?

   a. One person goes to a butcher to buy meat, while another person goes to a supermarket.
   b. One person loves to sail while another person gets seasick at the sight of a boat.
   c. One person like meat and another person likes poison.
   d. A detective finds poisoned meat at the scene of a crime.

7. "Don't count your chickens before they hatch." This proverb means that you cannot be sure of getting something until you have it in your hands. In which situation could you use this proverb?

   a. Someone drops a dozen eggs and breaks them.
   b. A man plans how to spend his prize money before he wins the prize.
   c. A fox eats all the farmer's chickens.
   d. Many people eat eggs for breakfast; those eggs will never be chickens.

8. "You can catch more flies with honey than vinegar." This proverb means that people will do more for you when you're nice than when you are unpleasant. In which situation can you use this proverb?

   a. Someone uses honey instead of sugar to sweeten a cup of tea.
   b. A bakery is full of flies.
   c. A customer is screaming at a salesperson in a store.
   d. A customer is asking for insect spray.

9. "Too many cooks spoil the broth." This proverb means that when many people work together on a project, they often disagree on how things should be done. In which situation could you use this proverb?

   a. One child is spoiling a game for all the others.
   b. Three mechanics are fighting about how to fix one car engine.
   c. A customer in a restaurant is complaining about the soup.
   d. Two students are studying for an exam together.

10. "A watched pot never boils." This proverb means that an awaited thing seems to happen more slowly when you are only thinking about and waiting for that one special thing to happen. In which situation could you use this proverb?

   a. A student has a long homework assignment.
   b. Someone's watch isn't working.
   c. Two people are relaxing and watching television.
   d. A student is looking at the clock, waiting for class to end.

Fables and Morals

A fable is a short tale or story that teaches a lesson or moral. Aesop, a Greek who lived from 620 B.C. to 560 B.C., is the author of many famous fables. The writers of fables often use animals or non-living objects as characters. The behavior of the animals and objects helps people recognize and think about their own funny or foolish actions.

Read the fables below. Think about the lesson each fable is trying to teach. Choose the best moral from the four possible choices at the end of each story. Write the moral on your own paper.

1. The Boy Who Cried "Wolf"

Once there was a boy who had a job taking care of sheep. It wasn't very interesting work and he was often bored and lonely. One day he decided to have some fun.

He began to scream as loudly as he could, "Help! Help! A wolf! Help me!"

The people from the town heard his cries and ran to help

him. They were carrying brooms and sticks and axes and were ready to kill the wolf and save the boy and the sheep.

The boy saw them running and he saw the fear in their faces.

He fell on the ground and laughed. "Oh," he laughed. "I fooled you. I fooled you. You all look so silly and scared."

The people of the town were furious and some of them yelled at the boy. They walked angrily back to town.

The next day the boy was bored. "I think I'll try it again," said the boy, and he began to scream for help. Again the people came running to save him. When they saw him laughing and rolling on the ground, one man slapped him and the others yelled at him. And they all walked back to town.

The next day the boy was watching the sheep. Suddenly a wolf came out of the woods.

"Help! Help!" he cried. "A wolf is killing the sheep!" But no one came and the wolf killed all the sheep.

The moral of the story is:

    a. You can't trust anybody.
    b. People are kind to liars.
    c. No one believes liars even when they tell the truth.
    d. People like to help others.

2. The Fox and the Grapes

One day a hungry fox went into a garden looking for food. He saw some ripe, juicy purple grapes hanging above him. He knew right away that the grapes were exactly what he wanted to eat. There was only one problem. The grapes were high in the air. The fox jumped as high as he could. He spent more than an hour jumping and jumping, trying to get at the delicious grapes. Finally he realized that he was unable to reach them. He walked out of the garden still hungry and very angry, saying, "Ah, I didn't want those rotten grapes anyway. They were probably as sour as lemons."

The moral of this story is:

    a. He who jumps highest gets the grapes.
    b. Don't go where you don't belong; you'll only get in trouble.
    c. Keep your eye on things that are high.
    d. Some people say they hate things just because they can't get them.

3. The Ant and the Grasshopper

One cold winter day a hungry grasshopper was speaking with an ant. The grasshopper said, "I know you have extra food; please give me some. I have nothing and I am very hungry."

The ant answered, "I worked long and hard all summer to save food for the winter. What were you doing?"

"I was busy singing and playing. I had no time to worry about work or the cold winter ahead," answered the miserable grasshopper.

"Well," said the ant, "you can sing and play during the winter, too, because I am keeping my food for myself." With that the ant disappeared and the grasshopper, hungry and cold, walked on his way.

The moral of this story is:

a. Be serious. You shouldn't sing in the winter.
b. Plan ahead. You can't expect others to take care of you.
c. Keep warm. You have to stay indoors in the winter.
d. Keep smiling. It's always best to be friendly when you need a favor.

4. The Rabbit and the Turtle

One day a rabbit and a turtle were talking. The rabbit said to the turtle, "You're the slowest animal on earth. I don't understand why you bother to move at all."

"Maybe I'm slow," said the turtle, "but I think I can win a race with you."

The rabbit laughed. "Fine," she said. "I'll see you at the finish line," and she ran off.

It was a hot day and the rabbit began to feel a little sleepy. "I think I'll take a little nap under this tree," she thought. "If Turtle passes me, it will be easy to run ahead of her later."

The rabbit fell asleep. When she woke up it was dark. Suddenly she remembered the race. She got up and began to run. When she reached the finish line, the turtle was waiting for her.

"Well," said Turtle. "I guess I won."

The moral of this story is:

a. Taking naps is a bad idea.
b. Never run a race with a turtle on a hot summer day.
c. Slow and steady wins the race. Speed is not always the most important thing.
d. Turtles are smarter than rabbits.

5. The Little Crabs and Their Mother

A mother crab was teaching her children to walk. "Walk straight," she said angrily to her children. "Stop walking sideways. You look ridiculous."

"Oh mother," said the children. "We want to walk straight. Please teach us how. Show us! Show us! Then we can learn from you."

But like all crabs, Mother Crab couldn't walk straight either.

The moral of the story is:

   a. Mothers are the best teachers.
   b. Don't tell other people to do things you cannot do yourself.
   c. Children who are disrespectful to their parents make their parents unhappy.
   d. Don't be angry with your children or they won't learn well.

6. The Wind and the Sun

The wind and the sun were arguing about who was stronger.

"Let's have a contest," said the wind. "Look down on the earth. Do you see that man walking on the road? Let's see who can make him take off his coat first. That will prove who is stronger."

"Fine with me," said the sun. "You go first."

The wind began to blow. Leaves blew off the trees and flew around in the air. "Do you see how strong I am?" asked the wind. He blew harder but when the man felt the cold air he pulled his coat tighter.

Then the sun began to shine. The heat from the sun beat down on the man and he began to feel warm. He finally took off his coat and sat down under a tree to rest.

The sun smiled at the wind and said, "Now who is the stronger?"

The moral of the story is:

   a. If you want to argue, you have to prepare to lose.
   b. Sometimes the gentle way is more effective than force.
   c. Heat makes you more uncomfortable than cold.
   d. People who think they are better are often losers.

Millie talks about . . .

TIPPING

A lot of people don't like to give the waiters extra money, you know what I mean—a tip—but maybe those people don't understand about waitresses and waiters. You see, we get very low wages, most of the time less than minimum wage. We count on the tips as part of our salary. Why, if waiters and waitresses didn't get tips, they wouldn't make enough money to live.

People ask me, "What's a good tip?" I like to get 15% of the bill. So if a customer has to pay $20.00 for her dinner, I like to get about $3.00 for a tip. Sometimes I expect 20% if I did a lot of work for the customer. For example, if I got her a special kind of food or a recipe from the chef. But do you know something? Very often it's the person you work the most for who gives you the smallest tip. Go and figure that out!

But to tell the truth, I do pretty well with tips. I'm kind of a friendly person so people usually like me. They talk to me during their meal and leave me a good tip. Of course some people prefer a quiet waitress and every once in a while I get some pretty small tips or no tip at all. Well, you can't please everyone, I always say. Some people like me and some don't. But now I'm forgetting about tipping.

You know the other waitresses and I looked up "tipping" once in a book about words. It said that the letters in the word "tip" stand for "To Insure Promptness." In other words, to make sure that we do things right away. The book said that no one knows if that is the real meaning of "tip," but it makes sense to me. If we know a regular customer is a good tipper, then we make sure he gets good service. But if someone gives small tips, we aren't in such a hurry to bring him his food or get his drinks. So remember, be nice to your waitress and she'll be nice to you.

Thanks,
Millie

Information, Please

Use facts from the reading and your own knowledge and ideas. Write your answers on a separate piece of paper.

1. What is a tip?
2. Why are tips important to waiters and waitresses?
3. What percent of a restaurant bill is a good tip?
4. What does the word "tip" mean?
5. Why do you think some customers don't tip or tip poorly?

What's the Tip?

According to Millie, how much tip is correct on the following restaurant bills?

	Good tip (15%)	Excellent tip (20%)
1. $5.00	_____	_____
2. $20.00	_____	_____
3. $100.00	_____	_____
4. $37.00	_____	_____

Understanding Proverbs

Sometimes Millie uses proverbs to say what she means. Choose the proverb that best fits each sentence and situation below. Write your answers on a separate paper.

1. Millie says, "Well you can't please everyone, I always say." What proverb could she use instead?

   a. "There are plenty more fish in the sea."
   b. "One man's meat is another man's poison."
   c. "Too many cooks spoil the broth."
   d. "The grass is always greener on the other side of the fence."

2. Millie says, "Be nice to your waitress and she'll be nice to you." What proverb could she use?

   a. "The squeaky wheel gets the grease."
   b. "A watched pot never boils."
   c. "You can catch more flies with honey than vinegar."
   d. "A friend in need is a friend indeed."

Cause and Effect

Read the situations below. What do you think happened before? What caused each situation? Write your answers on a separate piece of paper. Use the information in the reading and your own ideas.

1. A customer leaves Millie a $10.00 tip. What do you think is the cause?

2. Millie doesn't like to wait on a certain customer. What do you think is the cause?

3. The waitresses are always happy to see Ms. Goodwin. They make sure she gets good service. What do you think is the cause?

Talking About You

1. Do you or does anyone in your family work in a restaurant? Talk about your experiences. What are the advantages and disadvantages of working for tips?

2. Do you like to eat in restaurants? What are some of your favorite kinds of restaurants and your favorite kinds of food?

3. In the U.S., people are expected to tip their waiters and waitresses. What other workers in the U.S. depend on tips as part of their salaries? How much should you tip those people? If you have lived in another country, tell the class how tipping is done in that country.

4. What proverbs do you know in your own language? Translate them and share them with the class.

Composition Corner

1. A "Dear John" letter is one way to end a romance. In the letter, the person writing gives reasons he or she can't be a part of the romance anymore. People usually try to be as kind as possible in a "Dear John" letter. Pretend you are Ahmad's boyfriend. Write a letter to Ahmad telling her that you are not going to be her boyfriend anymore. Give all your reasons for ending the romance. Remember, you are trying to be nice and not hurt her feelings.

2. Write your own fable. You may wish to use animals or non-living objects as your characters. Remember, you want to teach an important lesson about life with your fable. It may be easiest to think of a moral first, and then make up a fable to go with it. If you don't want to make up your own story, you can retell a fable you know from your own language. Do not retell any of the fables included in this lesson.

Who is Otto's secret admirer? Read the next story and find out.

Otto Fox was home alone. He was correcting some compositions from his English class. He began to read Juli's paper.

In my country birthdays are only for children. On a child's birthday, he or she is the most important person in the house. No one can say anything bad to the birthday person, and everyone does what the birthday person asks. The family celebrates the birthday all day long. The lucky boy or girl gets gifts, special food, and money. Birthday children don't have to go to school on their birthdays. It's a wonderful day. On the other hand, these celebrations last only until a person is sixteen. After that there are no more gifts or parties. In my country, birthday celebrations are not for adults at all.

"Hmm. Very interesting," thought Otto. "I'll give her a B+." Otto read Tin-Sek's paper next.

Birthday celebrations in my country are not like the ones here in the United States. In my country we celebrate the first birthday of a baby 30 days after it's born. The next birthday comes when the baby is one year old. After that, however, birthdays are not very important. There are no parties or presents like here in the United States. Sometimes there is a special chicken dinner and the birthday person eats the drumstick, or chicken leg, as a treat. The only important birthday celebration is for older people. If you are a man, your 60th birthday is the cause for a big celebration. A woman has her big party on her 61st birthday. The whole family, children, grandchildren, and nephews and nieces come to celebrate. It is an important day.

Otto put Tin-Sek's paper down. He thought, "My birthday is coming soon. I'll be thirty-five years old. I live alone in this small apartment. I eat dinner alone most nights. I only have Sandy, my dog, for company. (Get down off that couch, Sandy!) Who will come to my birthday party when I'm sixty."

Otto got up from his desk and began to walk around. He thought, "I have always been so happy. I have always had so much to do. Just recently I've begun to feel that there is something missing from my life." Otto looked out of the window at the black nighttime sky. He thought about old friends, his parents, and his college days. Finally he walked back to his desk and sat down. "I've wasted enough time feeling sorry for myself. I might as well correct these papers. Work will take my mind off these problems," he thought.

As he picked up the compositions from his desk, he noticed a red envelope sticking out from under a pile of bills and old letters. "What's this?" he said to himself. "Oh, I remember." He opened the envelope and read the card that was inside. "My secret admirer." He smiled sadly. "At least somebody cares about me. I wonder who it is . . ." Otto stared at the card for a moment. "You know, that handwriting looks familiar. I wonder if . . . No, it couldn't be . . . But who else . . . ? Now wait a minute! I know she has written me a couple of notes at school. I think I have one here somewhere. I'll compare the handwriting."

Otto opened the top drawer of his desk and began to look for the note. His hands were shaking. "Here it is, and the writing is exactly the same. Sabrina Goodwin is my secret admirer! I can't believe it! Sandy, can you believe it? Sandy, you know what I'm going to do? I'm going to call her up. I'll ask her out. Maybe we'll have dinner next Friday. I feel better already. Maybe it will be a great birthday after all."

What's in the Story?

Answer these questions about "Mr. Fox's Birthday." Use complete sentences and write on your own paper. You can find the answers in the story.

1. What was Otto doing at home that evening?
2. Who are birthday celebrations for in Juli's country?
3. How are birthdays celebrated in Juli's country?
4. When is a baby's first birthday celebrated in Tin-Sek's country?
5. What is the most important birthday for a man in Tin-Sek's country? What is the most important birthday for a woman?
6. Who was Otto talking to as he thought about his life?
7. What did Otto find on his desk?
8. Who is Otto's secret admirer?
9. How did he discover who she is?
10. What does Otto decide to do?

What Do You Think?

Use the story and your own ideas to answer these questions. Write on your own paper.

1. In the story, why is Otto depressed?
2. Do you think that Otto has an exciting life? Why or why not?
3. Why does Otto talk to his dog?
4. How does Otto feel when he finds out who his secret admirer is?
5. Why does Otto think it may be a great birthday after all?

 88 *Mr. Fox's Birthday*

Personality Traits

When you are reading, it is important to be able to describe what kind of person each character is. Words like *funny, shy,* and *friendly* describe people. These words are personality trait words.

Below are several personality traits and their definitions. On your paper, answer the questions about the different personality traits.

1. A lazy person is a person who doesn't like to work or use much energy. On a busy Saturday morning when everyone in the family is cleaning the house, you can find a lazy person:

    a. running around the block
    b. sleeping on the sofa
    c. cleaning the oven
    d. playing baseball

2. A studious person is someone who loves to study and learn. A studious person enjoys being in:

    a. the schoolyard
    b. the soccer field
    c. the library
    d. a restaurant

3. A grouchy person is someone who becomes angry easily. Everything bothers a grouchy person and he or she often says mean or insulting things. A grouchy person probably has:

    a. a lot of close friends
    b. a bad reputation
    c. a good job
    d. a happy life

4. A polite person is careful to respect the rights of others. A polite person lets others take their turns first, and speaks respectfully to other people. Which of the following are the words of a polite person?

    a. I was here first. Go away!
    b. I don't understand this. You're not teaching it right.
    c. What do you want?
    d. Excuse me, someone said that you wanted to see me.

5. An athletic person is interested in sports. Athletic people keep their bodies in shape. They usually play more than one sport well. Which of the following is the best gift for an athletic person?

    a. a box of chocolates
    b. tickets to an opera
    c. membership in a health club
    d. a painting

6. A kind person is interested in other people's feelings. Kind people don't want to hurt anyone. Which of the following is NOT the action of a kind person?

a. sharing his or her dessert with someone else

b. talking with a shy person at a party

c. parking in a handicapped space because it's close to the store

d. helping an old person across the street

7. Enthusiastic people are excited and happy about the good things in their lives. They are full of energy and have lots of plans. Which of the following are the words of an enthusiastic person?

    a. "I hope she's not mad at me."

    b. "That sounds terrific! Let's do it."

    c. "I'm freezing! I want to go home."

    d. "We'll never finish! There's too much to be done."

8. A moody person is someone whose feelings change quickly. One day the person is happy and friendly, the next day he or she is sad and depressed. Which of the following word pairs best describes a moody person?

    a. nice and pretty

    b. sad and unhappy

    c. blue and green

    d. up and down

What Kind of People Are They?

    You can tell a lot about people from what they say or do. Read the following paragraphs and decide what kind of person is being described. Use the personality trait words listed and defined below. Write your answers on your paper.

creative – A creative person always has lots of clever, new, interesting ideas.

energetic – An energetic person likes to be active all the time and do lots of things.

honest – Honest people think that the truth is very important. They don't lie, steal, or cheat.

loyal – A loyal person believes in someone or something and remains faithful and true.

patient –Patient people are calm and understanding. They don't get angry quickly and they try to understand other people's problems.

stubborn – Stubborn people think that their way is the only way to do something. They do not want to listen to the opinions of others.

1. Pedro sleeps only six hours a night. He goes to school full-time and works part-time in the afternoons. At night he plays soccer or basketball. He's seldom tired and his favorite way to relax is to jog two or three miles.

   What kind of person is Pedro?

2. Mr. Miller was teaching his fourth grade class how to divide. The students didn't understand. He had to repeat his lesson and explain the idea more slowly. Some students began to understand, but many others didn't. Over the next few days Mr. Miller explained and explained the lesson. He used many different ideas and words until almost the whole class understood and knew how to divide.

   What kind of teacher is Mr. Miller?

3. People in the High Street neighborhood don't buy their fruits and vegetables in the supermarket. They buy them from Mr. Martelli's truck. You can trust Mr. Martelli. He never tries to sell any bad or unripe fruit. His prices are fair. Anyone who buys from Mr. Martelli is a satisfied customer.

   What kind of person is Mr. Martelli?

4. Jake and Charles ran into the classroom. Each one saw the chair he wanted to sit in. Unfortunately, it was the same chair. They both sat down at the same time. Each of them had half a chair. Charles said he was there first and tried to push Jake off the chair. Jake said he was first. Both boys refused to move.

   "All right, boys," said the teacher. "If you won't move, then you can sit like that for the whole period." Jake and Charles sat like that for the whole period until the bell rang. When they stood up they were stiff and sore.

   "I don't care," said Jake. "I was there first."

   What kind of person is Jake?

5. Room 46A at Travis High School was always the dirtiest room in the school. Many of the students threw papers on the floor or left them on the desks. One day, Mrs. Duke had an idea. She fastened a basketball hoop over the wastebasket. Now the students love to practice throwing their papers into the basket. When they miss, they pick the paper up and try again. And that was the end of the problem.

   What kind of person is Mrs. Duke?

6. "Your school's basketball team has lost every game," said Jim. "They're the worst team in the city. I really don't see why you go to every game. It can't be fun to see them lose every week."

"You're right," said Margie. "It is disappointing; but I love our school and the players need to know that the students care. I plan to go to every game, win or lose."

What kind of person is Margie?

What kind of person are you? You can find out with . . . .

THE CHINESE HOROSCOPE

The Chinese calendar contains cycles of twelve years. A different animal represents each year. The first year of the cycle is the year of the rat. After that comes the year of the ox, the year of the tiger, the rabbit, the dragon, the snake, the horse, the goat, the monkey, the rooster, the dog and the pig. After the pig the cycle begins again.

No one actually knows why the Chinese named the years in honor of these animals but there are several interesting legends which explain the cycle of animals.

One story is that once, long ago, a Chinese King invited all the animals to his palace to celebrate the New Year. Only twelve animals accepted the invitation and came to the party. The first animal to arrive was the rat and the next was the ox. The other ten animals came soon after. To reward the animals, the King named a year for each animal.

Now many people say that if a person is born in the year of a certain animal he or she is like that animal. Find the year of your birth on the illustration and then read about the animal your year is named for. Don't be angry if your year is a snake or a horse or a pig. In the Chinese horoscope all the animals are wise and important. No animal of the horoscope is considered dumb or ugly or evil. The Chinese symbols or characters in the center of the illustration mean "birth" and "alike." They are pronounced *sheng* and *xiao* in Chinese.

The **Rat** – You are imaginative and charming. However, you get angry easily and can be very critical. You take advantage of every opportunity that comes along. You will do well as a photographer, a journalist, or a businessperson.

The **Ox** – You are a natural leader and other people have confidence in you. You work well with your hands. Stop thinking that you are better than other people. Don't always demand your own way. You will be successful as a surgeon, a general, or a hairdresser.

The **Tiger** – You are sensitive and capable of great love. Sometimes you can be very stubborn if you think you are right about something. You will do well as an actor, explorer, or animal trainer.

The **Rabbit** – You are a person people like to be with. You are loving and kind. Sometimes you are sentimental, but you are careful and will make a good social worker, diplomat, or nurse.

The **Dragon** – You are very popular because of your energy and enthusiasm. You are intelligent and like everything to be perfect. Sometimes you are too critical of other people. You will be a good computer programmer, businessperson, or politician.

The Snake – You are wise and charming, romantic and intelligent. Try to be more generous with your money and keep your sense of humor about life. You will be good as a teacher, writer, or psychologist.

The Horse – You are a very independent and hardworking person. You are intelligent, but you can also be selfish and conceited. You will do well as a scientist, poet, or engineer.

The Goat – You can be an enjoyable companion after people get to know you, but you often make a bad first impression. You are elegant and artistic and love money and the things money can buy. You must learn to complain and worry less. You will do well as an architect, a designer, or a director.

The Monkey – You are very intelligent and quick. You are popular, but you must be careful not to use other people. You will do well at anything you try to do.

The Rooster – You work hard and make decisions easily. You are a dreamer, love to dress in bright, fancy clothes and spend a lot of money. You will do well as a restaurant owner, entertainer or tour guide.

The Dog – You are loyal and honest. You learn very quickly. You will be happy as a secretary, mechanic, or vice-president.

The Pig – You will never disappoint others. You are honest and faithful. However, you worry and criticize too much. You will do well as a salesperson, an accountant, or a publisher.

Information, Please

Use facts from the reading and your own knowledge and ideas. Write your answers on a separate piece of paper.

1. How many animals are there in the Chinese horoscope?
2. What animal comes fifth in the Chinese horoscope?
3. Why did the Chinese King invite all the animals to his palace?
4. Who was the first animal to arrive?
5. Name four animals that did not accept the Chinese King's invitation.
6. Which animal represents the year of your birth? Which animal represents this year?

Personality Traits

Some personality traits discussed in this unit are listed below.

athletic	enthusiastic	humorous	loyal	sensitive
charming	friendly	independent	moody	shy
creative	generous	intelligent	patient	stingy
critical	grouchy	kind	polite	stubborn
energetic	honest	lazy	romantic	studious

1. Write the five words that best describe your personality.
2. Choose and write the three personality traits that you find most important in a friend.
3. Choose and write the three personality traits you find most important in a teacher.
4. Read the Chinese horoscope again. Which of the twelve animal descriptions fits you best?

Fact or Opinion

Read the sentences below. On your paper, write "Fact" after the numbers of the statements that are facts. Write "Opinion" after the numbers of the statements that are opinions.

1. 1985 is the Chinese year of the Ox.
2. It is a good idea to check your horoscope before making a big decision.
3. Many American newspapers print a daily or weekly horoscope.
4. An honest person will usually tell the truth.
5. It is ridiculous to pay attention to horoscope predictions.

Drawing Conclusions

Study the five personality traits you chose to describe yourself in the "personality traits" exercise above. Then think of two or three careers that appeal to you. Write one or two paragraphs explaining why each career would be a good choice for someone with your personality traits.

Talking About You

1. Are you like the description your horoscope gave? Why or why not? Do you like the career choices it offered you? Why or why not?

2. Are you anyone's secret admirer? You probably want to keep that a secret if it's someone in class, but think of people you admire from the world of television, sports, film, or the news. Tell why you admire the person you have chosen.

Composition Corner

1. What personality traits are important to you in a friend? Why? What personality traits would you look for in a boyfriend or girlfriend? What are the things you cannot accept in a person? What are some things you dislike, but can live with? Write a composition about these ideas.

2. Birthday celebrations differ from country to country and from family to family. Are birthdays important in your family? How do you celebrate your birthday? Write about the traditions and customs of birthdays that you are most familiar with. If you don't celebrate birthdays at all in your culture, write about another time when the family gets together to celebrate.

12. THE TELEPHONE CALL

Sometimes things aren't as easy as one expects them to be. Find out what happens when Otto tries to call Ms. Goodwin on the phone.

OTTO: Hello, May I speak to Ms. Goodwin, please.

VOICE: Who? Oh you mean Sabrina. Who's calling?

OTTO: I'm one of the teachers from the English Learning Center.

VOICE: Oh, was Sabrina a bad girl in school today?

OTTO:	Well, really! Who's speaking, please?
VOICE:	This is Celeste, Sabrina's roommate.
OTTO:	Oh. Well, hello, Celeste. Is Ms. Goodwin, I mean Sabrina, home?
CELESTE:	Oh yes. She's here.
OTTO:	May I speak to her?
CELESTE:	Are you a friend of hers?
OTTO:	Sabrina and I are acquaintances from work. She's my supervisor.
CELESTE:	Your supervisor? Which one are you?
OTTO:	I'm Otto Fox. What do you mean, which one am I?
CELESTE:	I mean are you the one who . . . Oh never mind. Do you want to leave a message?
OTTO:	Celeste, you said that Ms. Goodwin was home.
CELESTE:	Yes, she is, but she can't come to the phone.
OTTO:	Why not? Oh forgive me. It's none of my business.
CELESTE:	That's all right. She's in the . . . .
OTTO:	I'll call back later.
CELESTE:	bathtub. Don't hang up. Sabrina will kill me if I ruin . . . I mean . . . I'm sure she wants to talk to you. I'll take the phone into the bathroom.
OTTO:	No, no. You don't have to do that.
CELESTE:	Sabrina won't mind. Just don't hang up. Oh darn. The cord doesn't reach. Listen, I'm running around here like a chicken with my head cut off. Why don't I have Sabrina call you back?
OTTO:	OK. I'll give you my number.
CELESTE:	Great! Let me find a pencil. There's one here somewhere. (There is a lot of noise and crashing.) Oops. I'm sorry! I dropped the phone. Don't hang up, I'm still looking.
OTTO:	Celeste? Celeste?
CELESTE:	I can't find anything to write with. Tell me the number. I'll remember it.

OTTO:	All right. Maybe that will be best. It's 555-4726. Can you remember that?
CELESTE:	Sure 555-7426.
OTTO:	Look, Celeste. I think I'll leave a message.
CELESTE:	That's a better idea.
OTTO:	Please ask Sabrina if she wants to have dinner with me on Friday night.
CELESTE:	Oh yes, she'll go.
OTTO:	How do you know?
CELESTE:	Trust me. What time?
OTTO:	I'll pick her up at 8:00.
CELESTE:	I've got it. I'll tell her. Bye.
OTTO:	Thank you, Celeste. Goodbye.
CELESTE:	Good news. You have a date this Friday night.
SABRINA:	What? With whom?
CELESTE:	Oh no. I can't remember his name!

What's in the Story?

Answer these questions about "The Telephone Call." Use complete sentences and write on your own paper. You can find the answers in the story.

1. Who is calling whom?
2. Who is Celeste?
3. Where is Sabrina?
4. Why can't Celeste take the phone into the bathroom?
5. What happened when Celeste was looking for a pencil?
6. Why did Otto decide to leave a message?
7. What was Otto's message?
8. What did Celeste forget?

What Do You Think?

Use the story and your own ideas to answer these questions. Write on your own paper.

1. What kind of person is Celeste?
2. Does Sabrina have a lot of dates? Why do you think so?
3. Does Celeste like Sabrina? Why do you think so?
4. What does Otto think of Celeste?
5. What is Sabrina going to say to Celeste?

What a Monkey!

It's an old saying that one picture is worth a thousand words. When you use a comparison, you are painting a word picture. If someone tells you, "My brother is like a bear in the morning," you have a good idea of how he acts. If someone else tells you that Emily was a mouse at the party last night, you can be sure that she sat quietly in the corner, not talking to anyone. You don't need details; the comparison or word picture gives you all the information you need.

You probably already know some common English expressions comparing animals to people. For example, someone who calls you a chicken is calling you a coward. Being a chicken means that you are afraid of everything and you run away at the first sign of danger.

The chart below explains some other English expressions using animal names to describe people's personalities.

Expression	Explanation
She's a monkey.	A lively, playful person. Usually a young child who can't sit still.

Expression	**Explanation**
He's a real turtle.	Someone who always moves very slowly.
She's such a sheep.	A follower; someone who can't think for him or himself.
He's being an ostrich.	Someone who "hides his/her head in the sand," and refuses to face problems or reality.
What a rat!	A mean, vicious person; someone who has done something bad to you.
She's such a turkey.	A foolish person; someone who does silly, absent-minded things.
He's a lamb.	A gentle, patient, understanding person.
She's a crab.	A grouchy person; someone who is often in a bad mood.

Now use the chart to answer these questions on your own paper.

1. In which of the following situations are the people acting like sheep?

   a. A teenager tells a small child to stop bothering an animal.
   b. A person is driving fast because all his friends do.
   c. Someone runs for president of the senior class.
   d. People are walking together.

2. If your boss is a lamb he or she probably:

   a. yells at you in front of other people
   b. yells at you in private
   c. will let you have a day off
   d. does not face reality

3. A crab's family probably:

   a. laughs a lot
   b. argues a lot
   c. is very happy
   d. is very calm

4. In which of the following situations is a person acting like a rat?

   a. Someone is visiting a sick friend in the hospital.
   b. Someone is looking at someone else's newspaper on the train.
   c. Someone is driving a car too fast.
   d. Someone is breaking little children's toys on purpose.

5. Which of the following people is acting like a turkey?

   a. Someone is listening to a radio.
   b. Someone is painting a wall with a toothbrush.
   c. Someone is eating Thanksgiving dinner.
   d. Someone is washing clothes at the laundromat.

6. If a person is like a turtle, which of these is most likely to be a problem to him or her?

   a. keeping the house clean
   b. learning a new language
   c. getting to school on time
   d. saving money

Don't Be a Crab!

Read the following paragraphs. What animal is the main character in each paragraph acting like? You may want to look back at the chart on page 100–101. Write your answer on your own paper.

1. Billy stole $5.00 from his mother's wallet. Billy's older brother, Tom, caught him and said, "Aren't you ashamed of yourself, Billy? Mom works so hard to earn that money, and then you steal it from her." Billy looked embarrassed and upset. He said, "You're right, Tim. I'm acting like a real _____."

2. Jerry has not been feeling well for weeks. He knows he has a problem but he's afraid to see a doctor. If he is sick, he doesn't want to know about it. His wife says, "Jerry, don't be a(n) _____. Go to the doctor. She can help you."

3. Buddy hates to wake up on Monday mornings. He doesn't speak to his wife or children, and he often yells at the other drivers on his way to work. Everybody stays out of his way at least until noon time. After that, he's all right. Buddy's boss says, "Buddy is a good guy, but on Monday morning, he's an absolute _____."

4. Mrs. Talbot was talking on the telephone. Her two-year-old son, Christopher, crawled into the kitchen. He opened a cabinet and found some boxes of food. He emptied cereal, rice, and crackers onto the floor. Mrs. Talbot walked into the kitchen and saw the mess. She said, "Oh no! I can't leave you alone for one minute, Christopher. You are such a little _____."

5. Alexander's mother sent him to the store. She needed some eggs to make a cake. On the way, Alexander stopped at the park to watch some girls play baseball. Inside the store, Alexander walked up and down the aisles looking at food before he bought the eggs. On the way back, he stopped to watch some ants. When he got home, his mother was furious. "Where have you been, Alexander?" she scolded. "You're as slow as a _____!"

6. Otto Fox called Sabrina Goodwin for a date. Celeste answered the phone and took a message. Unfortunately, she forgot the name of the person who called! Sabrina was very angry with her roommate. She said, "Celeste, you're such a _____!"

The next time you use the telephone, think about the man who made it possible . . .

ALEXANDER GRAHAM BELL

Did you know that the man who invented the telephone wanted to be a concert pianist? Did you know that as a boy he gave himself his own middle name and invented a talking robot? It's true. As a boy, Alexander Graham Bell was so interested in speech and sound that he even taught his dog to speak!

Alexander Graham Bell's father and grandfather were speech teachers. They told Alexander and his brother Melville about their studies. Often the boys helped their father give lectures and demonstrations about his work in speech and pronunciation. When adults visited Mr. Bell, the boys talked with them about their father's work. Alexander liked talking with one of his father's visitors very much. His name was Mr. Graham. It was after this man visited the Bell house that Alexander chose Graham to be his middle name.

Another of Mr. Bell's visitors gave Alexander the idea for a talking robot. The visitor brought a book about an inventor who built a talking robot. Alexander and his brother were very interested in the idea. They decided to build a talking robot themselves. They used a human skull from Alexander's biology collection for the head of their robot. They made rubber lips and a throat to complete the head. The boys found that if they blew air up through the throat, and out the rubber mouth, the robot made sounds. The sounds were like a baby talking and crying. They were so real that they confused everyone in the house.

Alexander was so delighted with the robot that he decided to teach his dog to speak. He found that by moving the dog's lips and teeth with his own hands, he could get the dog to speak. Everyone in the neighborhood was amazed at the dog who could ask, "How are you, grandma?"

All of these things happened when Alexander was quite young. When he was fourteen, he left his home in Scotland to live in London with his grandfather. Alexander's grandfather sent him to one of the finest schools in London. When Alexander returned home at sixteen, he was able to get a job teaching music and speech at a local high school. In addition to teaching, Alexander also attended classes at the university.

Soon all the activity became too hard for Alexander. He became quite sick. His doctor told the family that Alexander needed a long rest in clean, fresh air. The Bell family moved to Canada. Alexander relaxed and recovered, but within a year, he was hard at work again, teaching and inventing.

Alexander Bell's new invention was a new experiment in speech and sound. This new machine wasn't for making sounds, but for carrying them from one place to another. After years of hard work, Alexander presented his creation to the world. It was the telephone—one of the most important inventions of the nineteenth century.

Information, Please

Use facts from the reading and your own knowledge and ideas. Write your answers on a separate piece of paper.

1. How did Alexander and his brother learn so much about sound and speech?
2. What materials did the boys use to build their talking robot? How did it work?
3. How did Alexander make his dog speak?
4. What were some of the things Alexander was doing when he was sixteen?
5. What did the doctor tell the Bell family to do when Alexander got sick?
6. What important invention did Alexander Graham Bell create?
7. Name three ways your life would be different if there were no telephones.

Figurative Language

Which expression would you choose to describe Alexander Bell as a child? Write the answer on your paper.
   a. As happy as a clam.
   b. As crazy as a loon.
   c. As busy as a beaver.
   d. As quick as a bunny.

Personality Traits

Look at the list of personality traits on page 90. Write the three words that best describe Alexander Graham Bell on your paper.

Following Directions

Try the following sound experiment, then write the results on a piece of paper.

Ask a friend to sit at one end of a table or desk and to tap very softly with his or her fingernails. Sit at the other end of the table or desk.

Can you hear the tapping?

If you can, is it loud or soft?

Now put your ear down on the desk and listen to the tapping.

What do you notice?

Why do you think that is so?

Talking About You

1. Do you use animal names to describe people in your language? What are some of the common ones? Are the personality traits of the animals in English the same as in your language or are they different? Give examples.

2. Have you ever noticed that when you're speaking a second language it's more difficult to understand someone on the phone than in person? Why do you think this is true? Discuss your ideas.

3. Suppose someone tells you that his brother acts like a bear when he wakes up in the morning. How do you picture the brother looking and acting? What animal are you like in the morning?

Composition Corner

1. Alexander Graham Bell began to prepare for his career as a young boy. Do you have any plans for the future? What are they? What are you doing now to prepare for a successful future? Write a short composition about these ideas.

2. Do you remember the saying, "A picture is worth a thousand words"? Here is a picture. Describe the picture. Write about everything you see. Tell what the room looks like. Then tell what happened. Tell what the man is doing and what you think he's going to do. Your story doesn't have to be a thousand words of course, but create a long and interesting one.

13. THE DATE

Will Celeste remember the caller's name? Sabrina is very upset. What will happen Friday night? Read the story to find out.

The Telephone Message

"Celeste, you turkey! I can't believe you!" Sabrina glared at her roommate. "Come on. You have to remember who called!"

Celeste scratched her head and thought hard. "His name was . . . now let me think . . . don't tell me . . . it was some kind of animal. Lamb? No, that wasn't it. Rabbit? No. I've got it! Wolf!"

"Not Arthur Wolf!" Sabrina groaned. "Oh Celeste, what have you done to me?"

"I got you a date for Friday night. That's what I did. You should thank me."

"Thank you?" wailed Sabrina. "Arthur Wolf is awful. I can't believe he asked me out. He hates having a woman supervisor and he's always very rude to me."

"Then call him back and tell him you're busy," Celeste suggested.

"I can't." Sabrina looked upset. "I don't really like Arthur but a promise is a promise. You've already told him that I'm going so I'll go. Maybe he's trying to apologize for being so rude all year."

"Yes, I'm sure that's it," said Celeste cheerfully. "He sounded so nice on the phone."

"Well, there's nothing I can do about it now," Sabrina sighed unhappily. "I just have to wait until Friday."

Friday Night

"I know you're going to have a good time," said Celeste enthusiastically. "You know it's funny that Arthur didn't mention your date at school this week. Maybe he's really shy. I can't wait to meet him."

"Oh Celeste, you don't have to wait around," said Sabrina. "I know you have lots of things to do before your trip tomorrow."

"Yes, I have a million things to do," agreed Celeste. "But I want to meet Arthur, too. The other things can wait. Oh Sabrina, there's the doorbell! I'll get it. You finish getting ready."

"All right. But Celeste, be careful what you say. One date with Arthur Wolf is enough; don't get me another one."

"Don't worry, Sabrina. I'll be careful." Celeste opened the door. "Oh, Mr. Wolf. Please come in," she said.

Otto walked into the apartment. He had some flowers in his hand. "You must be Celeste," he said.

"That's right. Sabrina will be here in a minute. She's getting ready."

Otto waited for Celeste to sit down, and then he sat on a chair across from her. "Have you and Sabrina known each other for a long time?" he asked.

"Yes," answered Celeste. "We grew up together in California."

"I've never visited California. I want to see it sometime," Otto said.

Celeste studied Otto's face while he was talking. "You know, Mr. Wolf, you're very different from the way Sabrina described you."

"Really?" said Otto. "You're exactly the way I pictured you. But Celeste, I want to tell you something. My name isn't Wolf, it's . . ."

Sabrina walked into the room. "OTTO FOX!" she shouted. "What are you doing here? I mean, what a pleasant surprise!"

"Surprise?" asked Otto. "I thought we had a date."

Otto and Sabrina both looked at Celeste. "Wait a minute," they both said at once.

"Now Sabrina," said Celeste quickly. "I told you I wasn't sure about the name. Wolf and Fox are very close. As a matter of fact, they're cousins in the animal kingdom."

"I'm afraid I really don't understand," said Otto.

"I'll try to explain," laughed Sabrina. "Celeste couldn't remember your name. She could only remember that it had something to do with an animal. To make a long story short, we picked a wolf, not a fox."

"Arthur Wolf? Why, he's the . . . Did you want to go out with him?" asked Otto.

"Oh no, not at all. I'm so happy that you're my date," Sabrina smiled.

"Me, too," said Celeste. "It's going to be a wonderful date. I can tell!"

Otto looked at Celeste, and then quickly at his watch. "Sabrina, we'd better get going. Put these flowers in a vase. I have a taxi downstairs and reservations for 8:30 at the Paradise Restaurant."

"A taxi?" asked Sabrina. "Oh, are you still having trouble with your car?"

"My car? Oh yes, my car. I'll tell you about my car during dinner. Good night, Celeste," Otto smiled. "It was a pleasure meeting you."

"It was a pleasure to meet you too, Arthur," said Celeste. "Good night!"

What's in the Story?

Answer these questions about "The Date." Use complete sentences and write on your own paper. You can find the answers in the story.

1. Who is Arthur Wolf?
2. Why has Arthur Wolf been rude to Sabrina?
3. Why doesn't Sabrina want to call off the date with Arthur?

4. Does Celeste have a date on Friday night?
5. Who is Sabrina's real date?
6. Why is Sabrina surprised to see Otto Fox?
7. Why does Otto say it is time to leave?
8. Where are Otto and Sabrina going to eat dinner?

What Do You Think?

Answer these questions. Use the story and your own ideas. Write on your own paper.

1. What kind of person is Arthur Wolf?
2. What kind of person is Sabrina?
3. Why didn't Arthur say anything about the date at school all week?
4. Why does Sabrina tell Celeste to be careful?
5. How did Otto know that Celeste was from California?
6. What are Otto and Sabrina probably going to talk about over dinner? (Name a few things.)
7. What was Sabrina thinking all week? How was she feeling?
8. Why does Celeste call Otto, "Arthur"?

Comparing and Contrasting

In this exercise you are going to read about how two people, places or things are similar. Use your inference skills (drawing conclusions, predicting outcomes) and your imagination to describe how the two people, places or things are different. Write your answers on a separate piece of paper.

1. Sabrina was glad that Otto Fox was her date and not Arthur Wolf. How do you think that Otto Fox is different from Arthur Wolf?

2. Bobby likes to fly kites. On Wednesday he was out for about 45 minutes flying his kite. On Thursday he stayed out all afternoon. How was Thursday different from Wednesday?

3. Tigers and house cats are distant relatives. They are both members of the feline family. How are tigers and cats different?

4. David and Robin are brother and sister. Robin must go to bed at 8:00. David can stay up until 9:15. Robin does not think this is fair, but her parents do. What is probably the difference between David and Robin?

5. Stephen and Anne are studying astronomy. Stephen reads the text book and studies for the tests. Anne reads the text but she also reads other books about astronomy. She buys a science magazine each month. She also bought a used telescope to look at the stars. How are Stephen and Anne different?

6. Two bags of groceries are the same size, but one bag costs $5.65, and the other bag costs $25.00. How are the two bags different?

7. In the year 2025, a spaceship leaves Earth. The people on board are searching for a new home. They find that humans can live on the planet Xeon, but not on the planet Krypton. What is the difference between the two planets?

8. Mrs. Watson is renting an apartment. Both 36A and 36B are vacant and they both have the same number of rooms. Mrs. Watson looks at both apartments and says, "Oh, I definitely want 36B." How do you think apartment 36B is different from apartment 36A?

*Otto and Sabrina have just become
players in . . .*

THE DATING GAME

One way to get a date is to call someone up and ask if he or she will go out with you. But in American culture today, there are many other ways to get dates as well.

There is the blind date. This doesn't mean that your date cannot see; it means that you never met your date before, and your date has never met you. You take a chance on a blind date. It may be wonderful; the person may be everything you ever wanted in a date. On the other hand, he or she may be the exact opposite of what you like. If you go on a blind date, you have to trust the person who is arranging the date, or "fixing you up." We call a person who is constantly "fixing people up" a matchmaker.

Adults can try to take some of the mystery out of the dating game by using a computer dating service. At a computer dating center people fill out questionnaires about themselves and about the kind of person they want to meet. The information goes into the computer, and if a person is lucky, he or she will get the names of four or five people who might be great matches.

Sometimes when two people are just getting to know one another, they go out on a double date. They ask a couple that they know well to go out with them. Everyone is more comfortable and much less nervous. Teenagers and young adults most often go out on double dates.

At one time men and boys paid all the expenses for a date. The times are changing, however, and now many people share the cost of dates.

Dating customs differ from one group to another in the United States, but one thing is certain. All over the country, people find ways to get to know one another and discover the feelings and beliefs that they share.

Information Please

Use the information in the reading and your own knowledge and ideas. Write your answers on a separate piece of paper.

1. List three ways Americans set up dates.
2. Which way sounds best to you? Why?
3. What is a matchmaker?
4. What is a double date?

What's the Message?

On your paper write the sentence that gives the main idea of this reading.

a. Everyone likes to date.
b. There are many ways of dating in America.
c. It's good to have a matchmaker as a friend.
d. In the U.S., you can ask someone on a date by calling on the phone.

Comparing and Contrasting

How is a blind date similar to a computer date? How is it different? Which do you think is the better way to get a date? Why? Write your answers on a separate piece of paper.

Figurative Language

Choose the best answer. Write the answer on your paper.

1. A person who breaks a date with a girl at the last minute in order to go to the prom with someone else is acting like a(n):
   a. monkey
   b. ostrich
   c. sheep
   d. rat

2. After the date, Sabrina asks Celeste what she thinks about Otto Fox. What do you think Celeste says about Otto?
   a. "He's a crab."
   b. "He's such a turtle."
   c. "He's a real lamb."
   d. "What a turkey!"

Talking About You

Discuss these questions in class.

1. In the United States and Canada many young unmarried people who are working or in school live with friends to save money. We call these friends who live together "roommates." How do young unmarried people live in your country or culture? Do they stay at home with their parents until they are married or do they live with roommates, too? Which way do you think is better? Talk about your ideas.

2. Some animal names in English are common last names, for example: *Fox*, *Wolf*, and *Lamb*. Others, like *Chicken* or *Cow*, are not. What animal names, if any, are common first or last names in your culture?

 114   The Date

Composition Corner

1. Dating customs are different around the world. At what age do people begin dating in your culture? Are some of the dating customs you have seen or heard about in the United States different from the ones in your own country or culture? Write about the differences and similarities between dating customs of your country or culture and those you know from the United States.

2. Suppose you decide to go to a computer dating service. The service gives you an information form to fill out. The last question asks you to write one or two paragraphs about yourself. You have to describe what you look like and tell a little about your likes and dislikes, your interests and hobbies, and your dreams for the future. On your own paper, write a paragraph or two like that, describing yourself.

14. DEAR DIARY

It's difficult to be the "new person" in a group. Olga is the new girl at the English Learning Center. The next story comes from Olga's diary. Find out what happens to Olga during her first month of school.

First day of school

I started school today; it was awful. The teacher was late, and I had to sit in the classroom all alone. There were other students in the room, but none of them spoke to me. They all seemed to know each other so well. A girl named Maria was telling the other girls about a job interview. She said she was so nervous that she forgot her own name. Everybody was laughing. A girl they called Juli kept looking at me, and I think she was going to talk to me, but then another girl named Trang began to tell a story about her cat. Everyone started laughing again, and they forgot all about me.

There was also a group of boys in the room. They were all bragging about what they did over the weekend. One of them, George, was talking the most, but then another boy named Juan walked into the class. He was all excited. He works in a fancy restaurant downtown as a dishwasher, and on Friday night he happened to come out of the kitchen and he saw the English teacher with a date. Big deal! I didn't even want to listen to his story, but he was speaking so loudly that I couldn't help it.

Finally the teacher arrived. He was singing and he looked happy, but he didn't even notice me. I had to raise my hand and bring him my white entry card and schedule. After he looked at them, he put me in the back of the room and made me take an easy test. I'm sure I got all the answers right.

When the bell rang to end the class, everyone left together— talking and laughing. No one asked if I knew where to go next.

Mr. Fox came to collect the test. I said, "That was an easy test. I hope that the class will be more difficult." Now why did I say that? Mr. Fox looked at me and said, "I'll find enough work to keep you busy, Olga." He wasn't smiling anymore. What am I going to do? How am I going to stay in this school? Why did I leave my own country? I was so happy there.

Fourth day of school

Today was a little better. Juli spoke to me and asked me if I had anybody to eat lunch with. She invited me to eat at her table and she introduced me to some girls from her country. Juli has had a very interesting life and she has lived in many places. She even speaks a little Russian. At least I have one friend at school.

Seventh day of school

I'm beginning to like Mr. Fox. He is very nice. I guess he forgot what I said to him on the first day of school. I'm glad. I don't know why I said that. I didn't mean to be rude. I was a little afraid that he was going to be mad at me and give me lots of extra work, but he's too nice to do something like that.

Ninth day of school

I almost got on the wrong bus today, but Tin-Sek, one of the boys from my English class, was at the bus stop and he showed me what bus to take to go downtown. He was going downtown, too. While we were riding on the bus he told me a funny story about his mother getting lost. He's such a nice guy. I feel terrible that I thought he was like the other boys.

Fifteenth day of school

Trang came up to me today and asked me if I like cats. This made me feel a little sad because I had to leave my own cat, Boris, behind when I came to the United States. Trang said that she found a homeless kitten in an alley near her home the other day. Her mother and father won't let her keep it because she has one cat, Strawberry, already. I went to Trang's house after school and saw the kitten. It was just beautiful. I called my father and asked him if I could bring the cat home. To my surprise he said yes. What a wonderful day! A new friend. A new cat. And I got an A on my English composition, too.

Twentieth day of school

Today was a half-day. The teachers had a meeting in the afternoon, so classes finished at 12:00. I was walking out the door when I saw Ahmad and Maria. They were laughing as usual. When they saw me, they looked at each other and called to me. They asked me if I wanted to go to their favorite restaurant for lunch. At first I wasn't sure, but they insisted. They said that they wanted me to meet a friend of theirs. The friend was a waitress named Millie. Maria and Ahmad said that she was very funny. I decided to go, and I'm glad I did. Millie was so funny that we never stopped laughing. She told us stories about her school days and her old boyfriends. At one point I thought that she was going to sit down at the table with us, but I know that a waitress can't do something like that. We told Millie that we'll be back on our next half-day. I can't wait!

Thirtieth day of school

I feel very excited. Mr. Fox has invited the class to his apartment for dinner tonight. He has some news to tell us. Each student is going to bring a special food, and Mr. Fox is going to cook, too. Ms. Goodwin, the supervisor, is also going to be there. She's going to help Mr. Fox with the cooking. I never imagined that I could be so happy here. I will always love my country, but I am also beginning to feel at home here in the United States. I can't believe that I ever disliked Mr. Fox and the students in his class. I guess I was afraid that they weren't going to like me.

I must stop writing now. George is coming soon to pick me up in his new van. He is such a good driver. He told me that he loves to drive except in the snow. He hates the snow. Well, winter is over anyway, and spring is here. I know that the rest of the year is going to be wonderful.

What's in the Story?

Answer these questions about "Dear Diary." Use complete sentences and write on your own paper. You can find the answers in the story.

1. How was Olga's first day at school?
2. Why didn't Juli talk to Olga?
3. Where does Juan work? What did he see at work last Friday?
4. What did Mr. Fox do when Olga gave him her entry card?
5. What did Juli ask Olga?
6. How did Tin-Sek help Olga?
7. Did the girls have a good time at the restaurant? Why?
8. Why are the students going to Mr. Fox's apartment?

What Do You Think?

Answer these questions. Use the story and your own ideas. Write on your own paper.

1. How does Olga change from the beginning of the story?
2. Why does Olga dislike everyone at first?
3. Did the students in the class ever dislike Olga? Why do you think so?
4. Who helped Olga the most? How was that person especially helpful?
5. Why did Tin-Sek tell Olga the story about his mother?
6. Why do you think Olga's father let her have the kitten?
7. Olga thought that the English class was going to be too easy for her. Was it? How do you know?
8. What news do you think Mr. Fox is going to tell the students at the party?

Understanding Words Through Context

When people read, especially in a second language, they often come across words they have never seen before. It is possible to guess the meaning of these words from context—the subject of the reading and other words in the selection. For example, suppose you are reading a selection about eye care and you see the sentence: *The man couldn't see without his bifocals.* You can guess that bifocals are some kind of glasses because of the subject of the reading—eye care—and the phrase *couldn't see*

without. Figuring out words through context allows people to continue reading with understanding even though they don't know all the words. Later, if they wish, they can use a dictionary to check the exact meaning and pronunciation of the new words.

Read the sentences below. Use the other words in the sentence to choose the best meaning of each word in *italic* type. Write the definition on your paper.

1. Ever since Mr. Williams became bald, he wears a *toupee.* A *toupee* is:

   a. a large hat
   b. false hair

   c. a dark suit
   d. a kind of jewelry

2. Please don't drop that package. The things inside are *fragile. Fragile* things:

   a. are expensive
   b. come in packages

   c. fall on the floor
   d. break easily

3. I can't fix this car without the correct size *wrench.* A *wrench* is:

   a. an animal
   b. a building

   c. a mechanic
   d. a tool

4. When the laboratory assistant opened the cage door, the mice *fled* in all directions. *Fled* means:

   a. lost blood
   b. bit fiercely

   c. ran quickly
   d. walked quietly

5. The two boys washed and scrubbed the kitchen floor until it was *immaculate. Immaculate* means:

   a. extremely tired
   b. extremely dirty

   c. extremely wet
   d. extremely clean

6. Franny *detested* her cruel boss; no one had ever treated her so badly before. *Detested* means:

   a. bothered
   b. hated

   c. killed
   d. loved

7. The teacher tried to *ignore* the whispering at the back of the room, but finally she had to ask the students to be quiet. *Ignore* means:

   a. to speak louder than
   b. to pay no attention to

   c. to speak more softly than
   d. to listen to

8. Mrs. Perez *scolded* her children when they walked on her clean floor with muddy feet. *Scolded* means:

   a. cried
   b. yelled at

   c. walked
   d. made dirty

9. Lisa only *glimpsed* the traffic accident, but she said it looked terrible. *Glimpsed* means:

   a. caused
   b. started slowly

   c. spoke quietly
   d. saw quickly

10. When the new company opens they are going to *hire* several hundred people from the town. *Hire* means:

    a. to give jobs to
    b. to take jobs from

    c. to help with
    d. to send to

11. Maria's parents are very *strict*. They won't let her stay out past nine o'clock or date until she is twenty-one years old. *Strict* parents:

    a. don't let their children get married
    b. obey their children

    c. have many rules for their children to follow
    d. make their children cry

12. The peaches will be *ripe* soon. They'll be delicious in a pie next week. *Ripe* means:

    a. ready to grow
    b. ready to cut

    c. ready to eat
    d. ready to go

13. My sister plays the *oboe* in the school orchestra. An *oboe* is:

    a. a game
    b. a musical instrument

    c. a conductor
    d. a sport

14. John has become *conceited* since he won that scholarship; he doesn't speak to his old friends anymore. *Conceited* means that John:

    a. thinks his friends are great
    b. thinks only about school

    c. thinks he is better than everyone else
    d. doesn't think at all

15. The girl fell off the ladder and *fractured* her leg. *Fractured* means:

    a. fell
    b. broke

    c. lost
    d. touched

16. Don't *slam* the door; I have a headache. *Slam* means:

    a. open carefully
    b. close quietly

    c. close with force and noise
    d. break

17. Don't come near me; this sickness is *contagious*. A *contagious* disease is one that:

    a. you can get from another person
    b. is unusual

    c. kills you
    d. is always serious

18. We have five different kinds of apple trees in our *orchard*. An *orchard* is:

    a. a kind of fruit   **c.** a fruit tree
    b. a vegetable farm   **d.** an area with fruit trees

19. Yesterday two men *mugged* an old lady at that subway station. She was upset because she had $75.00 in her wallet. *Mugged* means:

    a. arrested and photographed   **c.** attacked and robbed
    b. beat and killed   **d.** stopped and helped

20. There's nothing like a cold glass of water to *quench* one's thirst. *Quench* means:

    a. satisfy   **c.** begin
    b. dry   **d.** quit

Using Context Clues

Read the following daily entries. Use your inference skills (drawing conclusions and predicting outcomes) and context clues to answer the questions about each entry. Write your answers on your own paper.

1. I spoke with James R. today. I told him he must be quieter in class. I corrected the quarterly exams; most of the students did well. The supervisor is coming on Wednesday. I hope the new bulletin board will be finished by then.

    a. What is the occupation of the person writing this diary?
    b. List five words from the paragraph that helped you decide your answer.

2. I love him so much. Everytime I look at him my heart fills with joy. He can't smile yet and he can barely open his eyes, but I'm sure he knows me. I love when he squeezes my finger in his little hand. Tomorrow we'll leave the hospital. I can't wait for all of us to be home together.

    a. What has happened recently to the person writing this diary?
    b. List five words or phrases that helped you decide on your answer.

3. I can't believe I'm going to be doing this for the next three years. We're up early every morning. We march or train or do exercises until we're dead on our feet. The food is terrible. The sergeants and officers yell at us all the time. I can't stand it much longer. Why did I ever do such a crazy thing?

    a. What did the person writing this diary do? (Where is he or she?)
    b. List five words or phrases that helped you decide your answer.

4. Today was a busy day. My office was full of clients. Some were sick and others were there for check-ups. At one point there was a little fight but the owners separated the trouble makers and all was fine after that. It is very quiet now that I have closed the office. No more barking and meowing until tomorrow.

   a. What is the occupation of the person writing this diary?
   b. List five words or phrases that helped you decide your answer.

5. The traffic was terrible today. It was hot too, but actually I had a good day. I had five trips to the airport and the tips were great. A lot of customers were friendly and wanted to talk. That helps make the time go faster.

   a. What is the occupation of the person writing this diary?
   b. List five words or phrases that helped you decide your answer.

Do you think Olga had a positive or negative attitude toward life? How about you? How is your attitude? To find out, take this . . . .

PERSONALITY QUIZ

Often a person's happiness depends on his or her attitude toward a situation or event. It is true that there are some situations that almost everyone thinks are terrible, but often a bad experience can be an opportunity to grow and learn. It all depends on your attitude.

Read the following situations and answer the questions *honestly*. Write your answers on a separate piece of paper. Then use the Scoring Chart at the end of the quiz to find out about your personality.

1. You planned an outdoor party and it begins to rain. What do you do?

   a. Cancel the party.
   b. Have the party indoors.
   c. Change the party to another day.

2. You lose a school election that you really wanted to win. What do you do?

   a. Congratulate the winner.
   b. Volunteer to help the winner make a better school.
   c. Stay angry for a week.

3. You get a bad mark on a test. What do you do?

   a. Throw away your paper and complain that the test wasn't fair.
   b. Ask your teacher for extra help so you can do well on the next test.
   c. Hope that you do better on the next test.

4. You are taking care of a small child. He spills milk on the floor. What do you do?

   a. Yell at the child and punish him.
   b. Make the child wipe the milk up himself.
   c. Ask the child to help you clean up and talk to him about being more careful.

5. One night, you cannot fall asleep. What do you do?

   a. Toss and turn and think how tired you'll be tomorrow.
   b. Get up and do some school work until you're ready to sleep.
   c. Lie in bed until you fall asleep.

6. You lose a book that you borrowed from the city library. What do you do?

   a. Never go to the library again.
   b. Pay for the book and promise yourself to be more careful with public property.
   c. Pay for the book but never take out a library book again.

7. You find that you have to repeat a subject in summer school. What do you say?

   a. "I hate it. I wanted to go away this summer and have fun with my friends."
   b. "Well, I was lazy this year so I guess I have to make up for it now."
   c. "I'm really going to learn this time. I'm going to be the best student in the class."

8. You lose your job and there is no other job available. What do you do?

   a. Decide to use the time to study and learn new skills.
   b. Spend more time with your friends.
   c. Watch TV all weekend.

9. A friend talks about you behind your back. What do you do?

   a. Get mad and have a fight.
   b. Feel hurt but don't say anything.
   c. Have a heart-to-heart talk with your friend and try to solve the problem.

10. Look at this illustration. What do you see?

    a. The glass is half-full.
    b. The glass is half-empty.

124   *Dear Diary*

Scoring Chart

On your paper, write down the number of points you received for each answer. Add up your score, then read the pesonality description after your score.

1. a – 1 point
    b – 3 points
    c – 2 points

2. a – 2 points
    b – 3 points
    c – 1 point

3. a – 1 point
    b – 3 points
    c – 2 points

4. a – 1 point
    b – 2 points
    c – 3 points

5. a – 1 point
    b – 3 points
    c – 2 points

6. a – 1 point
    b – 3 points
    c – 2 points

7. a – 1 point
    b – 2 points
    c – 3 points

8. a – 3 points
    b – 2 points
    c – 1 point

9. a – 1 point
    b – 2 points
    c – 3 points

10. a – 3 points
    b – 1 point

Your Personality Score

10–15   You are a pessimist. You look on the dark side of life. Your negative attitude is probably making life more difficult for you than it has to be. Try to be more positive and cheerful.

16–24   You are in the middle. You are probably more positive than negative and you try to make the best of a bad situation. You probably enjoy life most of the time.

25–30   You are an optimist. You're ready to make the best of any situation—good or bad! You will probably have lots of friends all through your life.

Understanding Words Through Context

Use the context clues in the reading to answer these questions. Write your answers on a separate piece of paper.

1. What is an optimist?
2. What is a pessimist?
3. Describe a negative attitude.
4. Who usually has a positive attitude, an optimist or a pessimist?

Compare and Contrast

Do you think you are more optimistic or more pessimistic than most other people? On your own paper, describe how your attitude is different from most other people's attitudes.

Talking About You

Discuss these questions in class.

1. What was your score on the personality quiz? Do you think that your personality description is accurate? Did most of your classmates get higher or lower scores?

2. Would you like to be more optimistic? Why or why not? Do you think pessimistic people are more realistic? Discuss your ideas.

3. Do you keep a diary or journal? What kind of things do you write down? Is it important to you that your journal is secret?

Composition Corner

1. Have you ever been the new kid in school? How did you feel? Were the other students friendly or unfriendly? Was there anyone who tried to make you feel welcome? If so, what did that person do for you? Write about your experiences. Tell how your feelings changed over time and why.

2. There are positive points and negative points about being young. Write about the good and bad aspects of being the age you are now.

3. Keep a journal of the things that happen to you for at least several days. Does your own life follow a pattern or is every day different? Be sure to put into your journal your thoughts and emotions about different situations.

15. SCENES FROM A WEDDING

You've probably guessed that Mr. Fox announced his engagement to Ms. Goodwin. Here's the story of the wedding day.

Otto Fox woke up with a start. The telephone was ringing loudly.

"Hello," he mumbled into the phone. "Oh, hi, Jim. Thanks for calling. No, no, I was awake. It's still early isn't it? Great. Come on over. We'll have some coffee."

"Celeste, Celeste! Wake up. It's my wedding day and neither one of us can afford to be late."

Celeste rolled over and opened one eye.

"Don't worry, Sabrina. We have plenty of time. It's only . . . 7:30?!! Sabrina, why didn't you wake me earlier? I have a million things to do."

"I've been trying to wake you up since 6:00 but you wouldn't get up."

"Well, I'm up now, so get out of my way. This maid of honor has to get ready."

"Well, Sandy, old boy, this is it. Just a few short months ago, I was facing my thirty-fifth birthday alone. Now I'm going to marry a wonderful woman. And you like her too, don't you boy?"

Just as Sandy was about to answer, the doorbell rang. Otto walked to the door. "I'm coming, Jim," he called to his best man.

"Now, Sabrina, it's not too late to change your mind," said Mrs. Goodwin, zipping up the long, white gown.

"Yes, Sabrina," said Celeste, "maybe you should wear your hair up instead of down."

"I wasn't talking about the hairstyle, Celeste. I was talking about Otto."

"Oh, Mother," began Sabrina.

Celeste interrupted, "Honestly, Mrs. Goodwin. Otto is the most wonderful person. He's so nice-looking and polite and kind and Sabrina says that he's an excellent teacher and all his students love him and they're all coming to the wedding . . ."

"Really, Celeste, it sounds as if you want to marry him yourself," said Mrs. Goodwin, glaring at Celeste.

"Mother, how can you say such a thing?" Sabrina scolded. "Celeste is just trying to help. What do you have against Otto anyway?"

"Oh, I don't know. It's just that everything is happening so fast. It seems like only yesterday that you were a little girl . . ." Mrs. Goodwin's eyes filled with tears. ". . . and now you're getting married."

Sabrina walked over to her mother and hugged her. "Don't be sad on my wedding day, Mother. You're going to love Otto as much as I do."

Mrs. Goodwin wiped her eyes. "Well, I don't know about that, but for your sake I'll try."

"Look how beautiful everything looks," whispered Ahmad to the other girls as they walked into Sabrina's back yard.

"I've never been to an outdoor wedding before," said Juli.

"Look," exclaimed Olga. "They even have a tent."

"It's absolutely lovely," said Maria. "All the flowers are in bloom and it's a beautiful day for a wedding."

"Do you see Mr. Fox?" asked Trang, looking around. "I feel a little nervous. We don't know anyone except Mr. Fox and Ms. Goodwin."

"Don't worry," said Maria. "Mr. Fox said that we'll all be at the same table. And we'll probably meet some new people."

"I know; but if people speak to me too fast in English, I get so nervous that I can't think of anything to say," moaned Trang.

Suddenly, the girls heard shouts of laughter coming from the tent.

"I can guess who that is," said Maria. "Who else would be so loud at a wedding? It must be George."

Tin-Sek, Alain, Juan, and George appeared at the opening of the tent.

"Where is everyone?" asked George. "We've been waiting in this hot tent for half an hour and nobody has come in yet."

"Get out of that tent," said Maria. "They'll only use that tent in case it rains. Come sit down at the table over here."

The boys looked at each other with embarrassment. They walked quietly to the table and sat down.

"Here comes Mr. Fox."
"He looks so handsome."
"There's Ms. Goodwin."
"She looks beautiful."
"I love her dress."
"What a beautiful veil."

"Do you, Otto, take Sabrina to be your wife?"
"I do."
"Do you, Sabrina, take Otto to be your husband?"
"I do."
"By the power invested in me by this state, I now pronounce you husband and wife."

"Congratulations, Mr. Fox. It was a beautiful wedding," said Olga. The students all gathered around Otto as the reception began. Otto looked at his students with affection.

"I'm so glad that you all could come and share this happy day with me. You're a very important part of my life, you know."

"Mr. Fox, where are you going on your honeymoon?" asked George, before anyone could say anything.

"Oh, didn't I tell you?" answered Mr. Fox. "I'm planning to teach summer school this year, so there'll be no time for a honeymoon." The students looked horrified.

"Don't listen to him," laughed Sabrina coming up behind Otto. "We have two tickets to Hawaii and we plan to use them."

"Same old Mr. Fox," laughed Maria. "Now that he's your husband, maybe you can do something about those jokes."

"Don't change too much, Mr. Fox," said Juli. "We like you just the way you are."

"Come on everyone," called Sabrina. "Otto and I are going to cut the cake."

As everyone began to walk over to the big table where the cake was, Otto and Alain remained behind.

"You know, you're a very important part of our lives too, Mr. Fox," said Alain. The two smiled at each other and walked quickly to catch up with the others.

What's in the Story?

Answer these questions about "Scenes from a Wedding." Use complete sentences and write on your own paper. You can find the answers in the story.

1. On what day does the story take place?
2. Who is Jim?
3. When does Celeste finally wake up?
4. What is Celeste going to do at the wedding?
5. Who helps Sabrina get dressed?
6. Where does the wedding take place?
7. Why is Trang nervous?
8. What were the boys doing in the tent?
9. Why did Otto and Sabrina have a tent put up?
10. Where do Otto and Sabrina plan to go on their honeymoon?

What Do You Think?

Answer these questions. Use the story and your own ideas. Write on your own paper.

1. How does Otto feel about getting married?
2. Does Mrs. Goodwin really want Sabrina to change her mind? What is she upset about?
3. How does Maria think that people should behave at a wedding?
4. Who says, "Do you, Otto, take Sabrina to be your wife?" What does Otto answer?
5. How do Otto and the students feel about each other?
6. Why do you think that Otto chooses his wedding day to tell the students that they are important to him?

Comprehension Review

The following exercise is a general review of the reading skills you have learned in this book. Read each paragraph carefully. Answer the questions on your own paper.

Pets can be good for your health. Pets provide company and friendship. They give people an opportunity for physical contact. They are loyal and trusting and love their owners without question. Scientists have found that frequent touching of pets can lower blood pressure. For many people, pets are a reason to get up in the morning. People need their pets for many reasons.

1. The main idea of the paragraph is:

   a. Pets can improve the health of their owners.
   b. Many people like animals.
   c. Dogs are good pets.
   d. Pets can lower your blood pressure.

2. According to the paragraph, what is one possible effect of petting and holding one's pet frequently?

   a. Waking up early
   b. Loneliness
   c. Lower blood pressure
   d. Sickness

Good nutrition is important for everyone. To insure that your body runs well, you need to get the vitamins, minerals and proteins that only a good diet can provide. Your doctor can recommend a diet that is good for you, but it is a safe bet that less sugary food and drinks, and more fresh fruit and vegetables are good for everyone. In addition, lean meat, fish, and poultry are good protein sources for most people. Watch your diet and you will probably look and feel better.

3. One conclusion that you can draw from this paragraph is:

   a. People who eat well never get sick.
   b. Doctors are always healthy.
   c. Too much sugar isn't good for you.
   d. Most people eat too much.

4. Which phrase would you probably use to describe someone who practices good nutrition, gets lots of exercise, and sleeps eight hours every night?

   a. As proud as a peacock.
   b. As sweet as sugar.
   c. As healthy as a horse.
   d. As good as gold.

Stamp collecting is a fun and interesting hobby. You can learn a lot from it. Many countries put historical events on their postage stamps. Other countries have such beautiful ones that they are works of art. In addition, finding new stamps from different countries is a good lesson in geography. Most philatelists agree that stamp collections provide hours and hours of entertainment.

5. A philatelist is:

   a. a teacher   c. an expensive stamp
   b. a stamp collector   d. an encyclopedia

6. Which of the following statements is not a good reason to have a stamp collection?

   a. You learn about historical events.
   b. You learn about world geography.
   c. You see beautiful works of art.
   d. You learn about the music of other countries.

When you send a business letter, you write your own name and address at the top of the envelope, at the left. You write the name and address of the person to whom you are sending the letter in the center of the envelope, halfway down.

The stamp goes at the top of the envelope, across from your own name and address.

7. Which of the following directions is correct?
   a. Place the stamp in the upper left corner of the envelope.
   b. Place the stamp in the lower right corner of the envelope.
   c. Place the stamp in the upper right corner of the envelope.
   d. Place the stamp in the lower left corner of the envelope.

The best things in life are free. Sunsets, warm summer days, and friendly smiles cost nothing. They are free to those who look for them. The next time you feel that you need money to have a good time, take a walk outside. Look at the unusual clouds in the sky, or look at the stars. Talk with old friends or better yet, make a new friend. Go to the library and borrow a good book. You don't have to pay for some of the most wonderful things that life has to offer.

8. On your paper write the sentence in this paragraph that states the main idea and that also is a common proverb.

9. The person who wrote this article is probably:
   a. cheap and miserly
   b. angry and negative
   c. happy and positive
   d. interested in free things

Always try to look your best when you apply for a job. Your future employer is making decisions about you from the moment you walk in the door. If you are messy or dirty, he or she may assume you are lazy and irresponsible. Employers agree that if you look neat and clean, your employer will have a positive first impression. Of course, appearance isn't everything. Your qualifications and interview are important too. Don't let a bad first impression ruin your chances on a job; always look your best.

10. Look at the following instructions. They are in the wrong order. On your paper, rewrite the instructions in the correct sequence.

   • Arrive on time for the interview.

   • Write a letter to the employer thanking him or her for the interview and restating your interest in the job.

   • Answer interview questions honestly and politely, and ask the employer questions of your own.

   • Get dressed neatly for the interview.

   • Before leaving, thank the employer for the interview.

11. Read the four statements below. On your paper write "Fact" if the statement is a fact. Write "Opinion" if the statement is an opinion.

a. A neat and clean job applicant will make a well-organized, responsible worker.

b. An applicant who dresses well is more interested in clothes than in the job.

c. An applicant who dresses neatly, speaks politely, and arrives on time usually makes a good first impression.

d. Your clothes and appearance affect how other people think about you.

Everyone should speak at least two languages. There is a great satisfaction in being bilingual. You can appreciate another culture and another literature besides your own. You can communicate with another group of people. When traveling, you can be more than a tourist. You can make friends and find bargains if you know the language of the country that you're traveling in. You'll have more opportunities if you know two languages.

12. One thing the article does not mention is:

a. jobs for bilinguals
b. appreciating another culture
c. enjoying travel
d. reading literature in other languages

13. In this paragraph the writer compares:

a. people who speak only one language with people who are bilingual
b. people who like to travel with people who prefer to stay home
c. people who like to read with people who like to shop
d. people who speak more than two languages with people who don't speak any language at all

Computers are becoming a large part of everyday life. We use computers now in school, at work, and at play. Not too long ago computers were for professionals only. Now many school children are taking introductory classes in computer operation. In supermarkets, computers read the prices of groceries and automatically record them. At home and in arcades, people of all ages play video games. Computers are a large part of our modern world.

14. Which two outcomes can you predict from the paragraph?

a. In the future, many children will learn how to use computers in elementary and high school.

b. In the future, students in elementary and high schools will be taught by computers instead of teachers.

   c. In the future, more and more people will use computers at work and at home.

   d. Soon computers will rule the world.

15. The main idea of this paragraph is:

   a. Children can use computers.

   b. At one time only a few people used computers.

   c. Computers are an important part of everyday life.

   d. Grocery stores use computers.

Otto Fox and Sabrina Goodwin did not see one another on the wedding day until the ceremony began. Mrs. Goodwin and Celeste both thought that to do so would bring bad luck. How do you feel about good luck, bad luck and . . .

SUPERSTITIONS

"Don't walk under a ladder or you will have bad luck." This is an example of a common superstition many Americans believe in. A superstition is a belief that has nothing to do with science or reason, but which has a strong effect on the behavior of certain people. For example, many people, like Celeste and Mrs. Goodwin, say that it is bad luck for the groom (husband) to see the bride in her gown before the wedding ceremony. This superstition probably comes from the times when parents arranged marriages for their children. The parents didn't want the new bride and groom to see each other before the ceremony just in case they didn't like each other and refused the marriage. As a result many husbands and wives-to-be didn't see each other until the wedding day.

Superstitions vary from country to country. Most people learn about superstitions when they are children, either from their parents or from other children. They grow up believing and practicing the superstitions they learn. As people get older and acquire more education, they often lose their belief in the superstitions of their childhood days. Still, they often like to obey the rules of the superstitions—just in case. For example, some people learn as children that spilling salt is bad luck. They also know that by picking up more salt and throwing it over their left shoulder, they can cancel the bad luck. Many adults continue this practice even though they say that they aren't really superstitious!

There are many other superstitions about bad luck. Opening an umbrella indoors or letting a black cat cross your path are said to bring bad luck. If you happen to break a mirror, American superstition warns that your bad luck will last for seven years!

One of the most common bad luck superstitions concerns the number thirteen. The fear of 13 is so strong that some buildings don't have a thirteenth floor. The floor above floor number 12 is called floor number 14. Many people think that Friday the thirteenth is an unlucky day. Some people refuse to travel on Friday the thirteenth for fear of a plane or train accident. Some people won't even leave their houses on that day.

There are superstitions that deal with good luck, too. Many people think that carrying a horseshoe, a rabbit's foot, or a four-leaf clover can bring a person good luck. Others feel that it's important to knock on wood to make sure that after talking about something pleasant or hopeful it will remain pleasant or come true. Some people put their faith in lucky pennies or other small objects that they wore or had once when something good happened to them.

Superstitions probably developed out of people's need to explain why things happened. Following superstitions may help some people feel that they can control the things that happen to them. Right or wrong, superstitions are a part of many people's lives, and many people believe in them enough to think twice before they do anything against the superstitions they learned as children.

Information, Please

Use facts from the reading and your own knowledge and ideas to answer these questions. Use complete sentences, and write on your own paper.

1. What is a popular superstition about wedding days?
2. Where does this superstition probably come from?
3. What are some "bad luck" superstitions? Try to include some that are not mentioned in this reading.

4. What things bring good luck according to superstition?
5. Why did superstitions probably begin in the first place?

Drawing Conclusions

Write the answer on your own paper. One conclusion you can draw from this article is:

   a. Only uneducated people believe in superstitions.
   b. Breaking a mirror brings bad luck.
   c. Things learned in childhood affect one's adult life.
   d. It is good luck to wear a rabbit's foot.

Understanding Words Through Context

The following sentences are taken from the reading. Using the context clues, choose the best meaning of the word or phrase in *italic* type. Write the definition on your paper.

1. Superstitions *vary* from culture to culture.

   a. are passed
   b. are different
   c. extremely
   d. are bad luck

2. They also know that by picking up more salt and throwing it over their left shoulder, they can *cancel* the bad luck.

   a. make less
   b. erase, get rid of
   c. stop believing in
   d. obey

3. Letting a black cat *cross your path* is said to bring bad luck.

   a. be angry at you
   b. walk on the sidewalk leading to your front door
   c. draw crosses on a dirt road
   d. cross in front of you when you are walking

Understanding Proverbs

Which of these proverbs is also a superstition? Answer on your own paper.

   a. See a penny, pick it up;
      All the day you'll have good luck.

   b. Early to bed, early to rise,
      Makes a man healthy, wealthy, and wise.

   c. Waste not, want not.

   d. Haste makes waste.

Talking About You

1. What are weddings like in your country or culture? Talk about what people wear. Describe the ceremony and the celebration people have before or after the ceremony.

2. What are some of the superstitions from your country or culture? Which ones do you believe in?

3. Are you afraid to meet new people? What kinds of things do you usually talk about when you meet new people at a wedding or other social function?

Composition Corner

1. Who was your favorite character from *In Good Company*? Was there one character you especially disliked? Write a composition about your favorite or least favorite character. Tell what happened to the character during the book and how he or she changed. Describe the character's personality and explain why you liked or disliked that character.

2. The boys were embarrassed when they realized that they weren't supposed to be in the tent. Did you ever make a similar mistake? Were you embarrassed? Perhaps you can think of some other embarrassing situation that happened to you. Write a composition describing an embarrassing moment.

Index of Reading and Communication Skills

SUGGESTIONS FOR USE
ANSWER KEY TO EXERCISES

*(The following pages may be removed before
the book is used, if desired.)*

IN GOOD COMPANY

Suggestions for Use

In Good Company developed out of the need, felt by both authors, for a reading text simple enough for most low intermediate students but interesting enough to make them want to read it, one that would at the same time build their enjoyment and appreciation of reading and build and reinforce a broad range of basic comprehension and word knowledge skills. It has been used in the authors' classes with hundreds of ESL students from a variety of backgrounds. The suggestions that follow are based on this use, and have been successfully applied to each of the fifteen units of the text.

Each unit opens with a short "motivator," two or three sentences to set the scene and pique the reader's curiosity. Begin the study of the unit by reading this aloud. Then have the students read the rest of the story silently. When they have finished, ask a few general questions: did they understand the story, did they enjoy it? Ask about the picture. Ask what's in it and how it relates to the story. Ask if the picture helped the students understand the story.

Then have the students close their books. Ask someone to summarize the story; ask others for specific details. After a few minutes of this sort of discussion, tell the students to open the books again to the beginning of the story. Read the story aloud to them as they follow along in their books. (Do not let a student or students read the fiction selections aloud: there is nothing more deadly than slow, inaudible reading!) After this rereading, highlight new or unfamiliar vocabulary, allowing those students who have larger vocabularies to define some of the new words. Be sure the whole class understands all the words in the story; clarify any definitions that are unclear.

The discussion of vocabulary should generate good, controlled conversation in the class. Do not interrupt the flow by switching to a writing mode at this time, even though many students may want to write. Instead, complete the first exercise, "What's in the Story?" orally. Students will try to write the answers. Discourage them from doing so even if it means prohibiting pens and pencils on the desk. At this time, you are teaching your students to answer questions completely and correctly: if they are writing, they can't concentrate.

Make sure the students answer in complete sentences. Don't worry about grammatical accuracy in their oral responses, but simply restate their answers correctly, emphasizing your correction(s).

Continue orally with the second exercise, "What Do You Think." To get the greatest benefit from this, be ready with supplementary questions. Do not accept yes or no answers: ask "why?" or "why not?" Ask what information from the story gave the students their ideas; ask them to explain or justify their answers. Get as much information as possible, but do so always in a supportive, friendly manner; be sensitive to personal areas that students may not wish to discuss. You will be pleasantly surprised to see how much most students do want to speak when given the opportunity. Most of the fiction stories include situations with which many students can identify. The "What Do You Think?" questions can be a real springboard for discussion of these situations and reduction of student anxiety.

You will probably want to stop after these two exercises. Now is the time for the students to write: assign the same two exercises, "What's in the Story" and "What Do You Think" as homework. Remind the students that they are to write their answers in complete sentences. You may want to review rules for the verb tense used in the chapter and any other grammar points that are relevant.

The following day, after you have reviewed the homework with the class, do the reading skill exercise that follows "What Do You Think?" Again go through the exercise orally before assigning it as written homework. Explain the directions for the exercise as thoroughly as possible, and ask students to explain them back to you. Make sure they understand such words as "main idea," "conclusions," "sequence," "fact and opinion," and so on. These are repeated frequently as skills are reviewed and should become parts of the students' working vocabulary. They are important terms because they are used both in standardized reading tests and in mainstream reading classes.

The nonfiction readings are somewhat more difficult than the fiction readings. They contain more difficult vocabulary, more formal grammar, and are more challenging conceptually. They are, however, thematically related to the fiction readings and in this way provide a thematic link with the familiar, which is helpful in motivating students to attempt more difficult material. You may decide not to use the nonfiction selection for a given chapter with your class or to limit its use to a more advanced group within the class. In most cases, however, with strong support from the teacher, students can derive a positive reading experience from the nonfiction selection. Refer wherever possible to the fiction readings and the reading skill exercises to prepare students to answer the "Information, Please" questions. When you present the review exercises (in all units except the first two), go over the skill orally before assigning the items.

The two final exercises, "Talking About You" and "Composition Corner" are completely open-ended, and no suggested answers are presented for them in the Answer Key. Questions in "Talking About You" are designed specifically for class discussion. Be ready to facilitate the discussion and to keep the conversation moving, but concentrate on getting students to express their own ideas. Don't allow one person to dominate; ask questions that bring in others (especially if they are from different culture or language groups). Remind students to respect and listen to each other. To help students to concentrate on the responses of others, ask one to repeat what another has just said; then ask another if he or she disagrees, and why. Let students know that you expect—and demand—their concentration and participation in the discussion.

When you tackle the final writing assignment, "Composition Corner," you may want to provide or generate from the class a topic sentence to get students started in their writing. Allow plenty of class time for discussion of ideas for compositions, but not for writing. Use class time to preview, teach, discuss, and review, not to write. Whole-class compositions done on a blackboard or overhead projector, however, can be helpful. Supporting a topic sentence is an unfamiliar concept to many students, and this is a good opportunity for them to see the process and participate in it with the support and guidance of the teacher.

Students' own compositions should be written at home. Students can and will write at home if they are adequately prepared in class.

In Good Company is written for concerned and involved teachers who want to challenge their students. Its use requires teacher involvement and participation: it was not written for students to use on their own. The kind of intensive support that we encourage you to give at the beginning of a student's reading experience will result in increased ability, confidence, and independence later on. We believe that the improvement you will see in your students' reading, writing, thinking, and speaking skills will make the work you put into In Good Company worthwhile. We hope you agree.

Anne Marie Drayton
Charles Skidmore

ANSWER KEY

NOTE: The following are suggested answers. Accept other answers if students can justify them. Many exercises ask students to answer in complete sentences. Because of space limitations and because there may be many equally correct "complete sentences" that answer a question, this key presents only the basic information that should be contained in the students' sentences. For example, the student's answer for the first item below might be, "It is December." The key, however, gives only the word, "December." Other shortcuts are used for the correct or suggested answers of other kinds of exercises: the letters of correct choices, fragments of sentences, etc. Many exercises are open-ended: they have many possible answers. For these, the phrase "answers will vary" is used, sometimes alone and sometimes with some suggested answers in parentheses.

Unit 1 — FIRST WITH THE NEWS

What's in the Story? 1. December. 2. cold, windy. 3. the teacher. 4. a student. 5. it's beginning to snow. 6. warm places. 7. he doesn't know the word for snow. 8. his bilingual dictionary. 9. Mr. Fox.

What Do You Think? 1. winter (late December). 2. No (he's not doing his work). 3. to tell the class about the snow. 4. story doesn't tell. 5. answers will vary.

What Happens First? A. e, c, a, d, b. B. Party:

f, c, d, g, b, e, a. Clothing: d, g, a, f, b, e, c. Letter: e, a, g, c, b, d, f. Shower: c, g, a, e, b, d, f. C. 1. b, g, f, a, c, e, d. 2. d, f, b, c, a, e. 3. e, c, f, d, a, b.

Information, Please. 1. difficult for cars and buses; slippery streets; loss of electricity. 2. tv and radio. 3. answers will vary. 4. answers will vary (vacations, holidays, weekends, etc.).

What Happens Next? d, b, f, a, g, e, c.

Unit 2 — THE LETTER

What's in the Story? 1. Rita, a friend back home. 2. her friends and the warm weather. 3. dirty wet snow. 4. students who are new to the United States. 5. friendly, and they do a good job. 6. English. 7. no one understands anyone else unless they speak English. 8. the class is small and Mr. Fox is nice. 9. it's a good thing English has lots of words because we have a lot to say. 10. early thirties.

What Do You Think? 1. her friend is learning English, too. 2. warm. 3. a little nervous; likes students to speak but not too loudly; likes students to be on time but is often late himself. 4. she likes them. 5. she doesn't think they're funny. 6. she's lonely.

How Are They Alike? 1. parts of the face. 2. vegetables. 3. school subjects. 4. books. 5. relatives (relations). 6. female relatives.

7. pets. 8. public buildings. 9. four-legged animals. 10. white things. 11. nationalities. 12. liquids. 13. bodies of water. 14. sounds. 15. words ending with double letters.

What's the Message? 1. d. 2. b. 3. c. 4. d. 5. b.

Information, Please. 1. 800,000. 2. 65,000. 3. scientists, doctors, lawyers; plumbers, mechanics, computer programmers, airline pilots. 4. 300,000,000. 5. U.S., Canada, England, Ireland, Scotland, Wales, Australia, New Zealand. 6. When they move to English-speaking countries; for business or travel; for fun and pleasure.

What's the Message? c.

Unit 3 — THE SUPERVISOR

What's in the Story? 1. 7:00. 2. the new supervisor is coming. 3. showers, shaves, gets dressed, feeds the dog. 4. 7:30. 5. $4.00. 6. $1.00. 7. the supervisor. 8. Ms. Goodwin. 9. 3:00. 10. where they can have coffee.

What Do You Think? 1. he wouldn't have to spend the time to shave. 2. Yes (it takes only five minutes to get there). 3. Otto's dog. 4. Otto's housekeeper (cleaning woman, dog walker). 5. talkative, confident. 6. answers will vary. 7. he needs an excuse for being late. 8. 7:30. 9. he has been late once that day. 10. Yes (they smile when he tells his lie; they perform well in class so that Ms. Goodwin compliments them).

Supporting Details. Answers will vary; be sure each is a supporting detail, not a restatement of the main idea or something unrelated.

Support the Main Idea: 1. b, c, d. 2. a, b, d, e. 3. a, c, e, f. 4. b, c, e, f. 5. a, c, d.

Information, Please: 1. wrinkled, bald, angry. 2. beautiful, perfect. 3. a lie told to make a difficult situation easier. 4. to be kind and considerate (answers will vary).

What's the Message? c.

Supporting Details: Answers will vary. Be sure each is a supporting detail, not a restatement of the main idea or something unrelated.

Unit 4 — STRAWBERRY

What's in the Story? 1. practice her English. 2. no (they don't speak English). 3. the other students know more English. 4. she walks. 5. the big signs. 6. it's breaking the garbage bags. 7. he's trying to kill the kitten. 8. takes it home. 9. to remind herself to practice English. 10. Strawberry (because she loves strawberries so much and is going to love the kitten the same way).

What Do You Think? 1. answers will vary (shy, courageous, loving). 2. answers will vary (cruel, unfeeling). 3. answers will vary (it's hungry). 4. she's determined to stop him from hurting the kitten. 5. he answers her. 6. she's had an unpleasant experience, but she has rescued the kitten.

Predicting Outcomes. 1. i. 2. j. 3. a. 4. c. 5. b. 6. h. 7. f. 8. d. 9. g. 10. e.

More About Outcomes: Answers will vary. Be sure students' answers are logical or probable outcomes and take into account the information in the paragraphs and do not contradict any of it.

Information, Please: 1. about sixteen (2/3 of 24). 2. 6 to 8 hours. 3. a short nap that a person takes. 4. answers will vary (so they can play with their owners). 5. because they sleep so much.

What's the Message? b.

Predicting Outcomes: Answers will vary. The cat's schedule will probably adjust to the nurse's.

Unit 5 — VALENTINE'S DAY

PART 1 — What's in the Story? 1. a day when you send cards and gifts to people you love. 2. have a party. 3. because he looks angry at the suggestion. 4. the first girl Otto Fox ever liked. 5. an expensive romantic valentine card. 6. 13. 7. "It was so sweet." 8. "I can't go with you . . ." 9. 34 (13 + 21). 10. an expensive, romantic valentine.

What Do You Think? 1. answers will vary (not celebrated in her country). 2. he was hurt when the first girl he liked turned down his invitation to a Valentine's Day dance. 3. answers will vary (someone else had invited her; he was too young for her). 4. answers will vary (he realizes it's silly to let an experience 21 years ago affect him now). 5. answers will vary.

PART 2 — What's in the Story? 1. happy. 2. he brought a cake. 3. get the drinks. 4. heart-shaped, pink frosting, pink and white flowers around the edge, "Be My Valentine" in the center. 5. it was too beautiful to cut. 6. ate and talked. 7. none. 8. no.

What Do You Think? 1. answers will vary ("I want you to enjoy Valentine's Day"). 2. answers will vary (he wants to be sure they don't make a mess). 3. answers will vary (they don't like him enough to send him valentines). 4. answers will vary. 5. answers will vary (married people get them too, often from their spouses but also from others).

Fact and Opinion. 1. F. 2. O. 3. F. 4. O. 5. F. 6. O. 7. F. 8. F. 9. F. 10. O. 11. O. 12. F. 13. O. 14. O. 15. F. 16. O. 17. F. 18. F. 19. O. 20. F.

Facts and Opinions in Advertising. Answers will vary. There are several facts in some of the ads, several opinions in some. Let students discuss and challenge each other's answers in class.

Information, Please. 1. chubby little boy with wings. 2. no. 3. romance. 4. Eros. 5. shoots them with his arrows. 6. makes people fall in love with animals or with people they hate. 7. cut himself with his own arrow. 8. Psyche.

Fact or Opinion? 1. F. 2. F. 3. O. 4. O. 5. F.

Predicting Outcomes. The person will fall in love with the frog. Answers will vary as to what the person will do.

Unit 6 — WHERE AM I?

What's in the Story? 1. her mother wasn't home yet. 2. chopping vegetables. 3. a friend and fellow-worker of Tin-Sek's mother. 4. two weeks earlier. 5. no. 6. his mother. 7. she took the wrong bus. 8. she described the gate, the smell, and the sound. 9. 45 minutes. 10. it's delicious; food always tastes better when someone else cooks it.

What Do You Think? 1. responsible, caring. 2. Mae Lee doesn't worry as much as Mae Ling. 3. answers will vary (Mrs. Lee has probably been in the U.S. longer and speaks English). 4. answers will vary (brave, dependable, OR foolish). 5. she always makes the dinner. 6. answers will vary (proves the responsibility of her children; gives her the chance to eat a dinner cooked by others).

Following Directions. 2. a. Joe's Pizza. b. buy a pizza. 3. a. Discount Clothing Outlet. b. buy clothing. 4. a. hardware store. b. buy hardware. 5. a. bakery. b. left on Summer St. to Franklin Ave. Left on Franklin to 4th building on right. 6. a. police station. b. right on Washington St. to Summer St., left on Summer to building on corner of Summer and Walden Sts. 7. a. library. b. left on Walden St. to Summer St., right on Summer to corner of Washington and Summer Sts. 8. a. post office. b. left on Walden St. to Summer St., up Summer to Washington St., right on Washington to second building on left.

Information, Please. 1. someone who disappears without any explanation. 2. as high as 250,000. 3. to escape problems and responsibilities. 4. find out where person was last seen; call friends, workplace, school; talk to neighbors and others; check what clothes and belongings are missing, call a hotline, call the police.

What's the Message: c.

Supporting Details. Answers will vary. Many sentences support the main idea statement.

Giving Directions. Answers will vary. A map of your community will be helpful in discussing and checking answers.

Unit 7 — GEORGE'S VAN

What's in the Story? 1. Tin-Sek, Juan, and Alain. 2. Juan. 3. at the movies. 4. Ahmad. 5. Ms. Goodwin. 6. a huge truck. 7. the truck hit the van in his dream. 8. not to drive fast.

What Do You Think? 1. answers will vary (they had to go home). 2. George wouldn't let the girls out. 3. answers will vary (she thought George would behave better with Ms. Goodwin there). 4. answers will vary (one time around the block wouldn't make the girls late). 5. schools aren't in session Saturdays, so there was no business reason for them to be together. 6. sardines are packed very tightly in a can; she didn't want George to hear her. 7. answers will vary (he enjoyed driving fast, wanted to show the girls he could do so). 8. yes; his heart was beating hard, he was sweating.

Something Is Wrong. 1. a. it appears to come closer and closer. b. it moved farther and farther away. c. they had no faces. 2. a. the dreamer became smaller and smaller until he/she went down the drain. b. answers will vary. 3. a. library and restaurant. b. answers will vary (Lucia's different face; eating books). c. answers will vary (happy: more confident about algebra; upset: test is still to be taken). 4. a. return to your seats and fasten your seatbelts. b. answers will vary (people caught them as they reached the ground). 5. a. the bullets didn't hurt him/her. b. happy; the soldiers have no power over the dreamer. 6. a. talks. b. answers will vary (baby acted older than 3 months, therefore could eat food for older children; baby had supernatural power over sitter). c. answers will vary. 7. a. Caribbean Sea is too warm for icebergs. b. lifted ship out of the water. 8. a. they wore black and were going to remove organs that he/she couldn't live without. b. person can't live without heart and liver. c. answers will vary (relieved that it was only a dream).

Information, Please. 1. 50,000. 2. when insurance doesn't pay the whole bill. 3. many drivers don't take driving seriously. 4. after drinking; when one is angry or upset. 5. always.

Predicting Outcomes. 1. answers will vary (they will protect you; keep you from hitting the windshield; hold you in place). 2. you can be hit by a car coming the other way. 3. a car behind you can hit you because the driver doesn't have time to stop.

Something Is Wrong. 1. change billion to million. 2. change minor to major. 3. change employees to customers. 4. change ninety to ten. 5. change difficult to easy.

Unit 8 — THE PROMISE

What's in the Story? 1. Alain. 2. his aunt and uncle. 3. stayed with his godparents and their family (saw his first movie, took his first airplane ride). 4. to attend his cousin's wedding. 5. in a plane crash. 6. she had a stroke. 7. when his uncle and aunt came back for his parents' funeral. 8. more than a year. 9. it's wonderful! 10. they began to applaud.

What Do You Think? 1. answers will vary ("How/why did you come to the United States?") 2. answers will vary (they were shocked/sad/sympathetic). 3. she was feeling sad for Alain. 4. unfortunate. 5. generous, kind.

What's the Effect? 1. c. 2. b. 3. d. 4. c. 5. b. 6. d. 7. d. 8. a. 9. b. 10. b.

Information, Please. 1. to show they like or approve of something. 2. theaters, concerts, football games, etc. 3. clap with the audience. 4. to show they did not like a performer. 5. standing up and clapping.

What's the Effect? d.

Something Is Strange. 1. change wave to clap. 2. change insulted to complimented. 3. change nightmare to dream.

Unit 9 — THE MISSING TICKETS

What's in the Story? 1. she was going to her first play in English. 2. the principal. 3. to give him the transportation passes. 4. Maria thought George was talking too loudly. 5. *Holmes, Sweet Holmes.* 6. a character created by an author from his/her imagination. 7. the top desk drawer first; then other drawers, his briefcase, his pockets. 8. $45 (9 × $5). 9. someone stole $2.00 out of her locker. 10. the teacher's room.

What Do You Think? 1. yells (talks, shouts, screams) as loud as possible. 2. answers will vary depending on students' perceptions and on whom they identify with. 3. he heard what she said and didn't like it. 4. she knew she had said something she shouldn't have. 5. answers will vary (he was too upset to think logically). 6. he just remembered showing Ms. Goodwin the tickets. (Slapping the forehead indicates one has just had a new insight or idea.) 7. to compare him with the detective, Sherlock Holmes; Juan's suggestion led to Mr. Fox's finding the tickets.

Drawing Conclusions. 1. Valentine's Day. 2. an animal (bear, etc.). 3. answers will vary (out of town, on vacation, in the hospital, etc.). 4. yes. 5. driver went through a stop sign. 6. answers will vary (friend, sweetheart, wife, child, etc. arriving on plane).

Are You a Good Detective? 1. at night. 2. chalk; a teacher or student. 3. arson (setting fire to a building). 4. the cup; to see if it has poison in it or fingerprints on it. 5. on the seashore (or lakeshore). 6. about 12:03 to 12:05 P.M. 7. valuable things were left behind: a thief would have taken them. 8. answers will vary (heart attack, stroke, "frightened to death," etc.).

Information, Please. 1. a successful doctor. 2. the Sherlock Holmes stories. 3. newspaper readers. 4. people with problems, police detectives. 5. answers will vary (jealous). 6. figured out some at home; looked for clues many places; wore disguises.

Drawing Conclusions. 1. answers will vary (people with problems, people who think Holmes is a real, present-day person; they have problems no one has been able to solve). 2. No. Doyle would be over 100 years old (he died in 1930). 3. b.

Sequence. 1. Arthur Conan Doyle started . . . 2. He wrote about . . . 3. He named this detective . . . 4. The first Sherlock Holmes . . . 5. The people of London loved . . . 6. Arthur Conan Doyle's stories . . . 7. Today people still . . .

Unit 10 — PLENTY MORE FISH IN THE SEA

What's in the Story? 1. a restaurant. 2. a valentine card. 3. coffee. 4. her boyfriend is going to marry someone else. 5. the Wonderland Ballroom. 6. he was handsome and a wonderful dancer. 7. in the summer. 8. Millie asked him to. 9. mad, sad, hurt, upset, and angry. 10. Charlie, her future husband.

What Do You Think? 1. answers will vary (she loved him, looked forward to marrying him, etc.). 2. they were having a private conversation. 3. about 50. 4. Ahmad will meet many other men and eventually find one whom she is attracted to. 5. a place where people went to dance when Mille was 16. 6. answers will vary (talkative, friendly, nosey, sympathetic, interesting). 7. she inserted herself into someone else's personal conversation without invitation and gave unsolicited opinions and advice. 8. she realized that her experience was not unique and that someone else was interested enough to care—and that there were "plenty more fish in the sea."

Understanding Proverbs: 1. c. 2. b. 3. a. 4. b. 5. c. 6. b. 7. b. 8. c. 9. b. 10. d.

Fables and Morals: 1. c. 2. d. 3. b. 4. c. 5. b. 6. b.

Information, Please. 1. extra money for a waiter or waitress (or other service person—taxi driver, barber, beautician, etc.). 2. they count on them as part of their salary. 3. 15% to 20%. 4. some people think it means "To Insure Promptness." 5. answers will vary (they have very little money, they didn't like the service, they are stingy or miserly, they are thoughtless).

What's the Tip? 1. 75 cents; $1.00. 2. $3.00; $4.00. 3. $15.00; $20.00. 4. $5.55; $7.40 ($5.50, $7.50 in round numbers).

Understanding Proverbs: 1. b. 2. c.

Cause and Effect. 1. answers will vary (he had a $60 meal; he liked Millie; she gave him special service; he had just won the lottery, etc.). 2. this customer tips very poorly. 3. answers will vary (she always tips 20%; she is always pleasant and never complains, etc.).

Unit 11 — MR. FOX'S BIRTHDAY

What's in the Story? 1. correcting compositions. 2. children. 3. everyone does what the birthday child wants all day; the child gets gifts, special food, money, and doesn't have to go to school that day. 4. 30 days after it is born. 5. 60; 61. 6. his dog (and himself). 7. the valentine card he received from his "secret admirer." 8. Sabrina Goodwin. 9. he compared the handwriting on the card with the handwriting on a note from her. 10. ask her out (to dinner next Friday).

What Do You Think? 1. answers will vary (he lives and eats alone, has only his dog for company, feels something is missing from his life). 2. no; all the above reasons. 3. there's no one else to talk to. 4. excited. 5. he'll have a good time with Sabrina Goodwin.

Personality Traits: 1. b. 2. c. 3. b. 4. d. 5. c. 6. c. 7. b. 8. b.

What Kind of People Are They? 1. energetic. 2. patient (creative). 3. honest. 4. stubborn. 5. creative. 6. loyal.

Information, Please. 1. 12. 2. the dragon. 3. to celebrate the New Year. 4. the rat. 5. answers will vary (any animals except the twelve in the Chinese horoscope). 6. answers will vary: see the circle illustration in this unit.

Personality Traits: Answers will vary for all four questions since all depend on student opinion.

Fact or Opinion: 1. F. 2. O. 3. F. 4. F. 5. O.

Drawing Conclusions: Answers will vary, but paragraphs should relate logically to the trait words chosen by the student.

Unit 12 — THE TELEPHONE CALL

What's in the Story? 1. Otto Fox is calling Sabrina Goodwin. 2. Sabrina's roommate. 3. in the bathroom. 4. the cord isn't long enough. 5. she dropped the phone. 6. Celeste repeated his telephone number inaccurately. 7. for Sabrina to have dinner with him Friday. 8. Otto's name.

What Do You Think? 1. a scatterbrain (disorganized, poor memory, happy-go-lucky, friendly). 2. no; Celeste is sure Sabrina will go out with Otto. 3. answers will vary (yes; she's interested in helping Sabrina). 4. answers will vary (thinks she's disorganized and scatterbrained). 5. answers will vary (she's going to be angry; she's going to call Celeste a turkey; she'll laugh).

What a Monkey! 1. b. 2. c. 3. b. 4. d. 5. b. 6. c.

Don't Be a Crab! 1. rat. 2. ostrich. 3. crab. 4. monkey. 5. turtle. 6. turkey.

Information, Please. 1. their father and grandfather were speech teachers. 2. a human skull and some rubber; they blew air up through the throat and the rubber mouth. 3. by moving the dog's lips and teeth. 4. teaching music and speech and going to classes at the university. 5. have Alexander rest in clean, fresh air. 6. the telephone. 7. answers will vary.

Figurative Language: c.

Personality Traits: answers will vary (creative, energetic, patient).

Following Directions: The sound is louder when one puts one's ear down on the desk. The material of the desk conducts sound waves.

Unit 13 — THE DATE

What's in the Story? 1. another teacher in the school. 2. he hates having a woman supervisor. 3. because "a promise is a promise." 4. no (she has "lots of things to do before your trip tomorrow"). 5. Otto Fox. 6. she expected Arthur Wolf. 7. he has a taxi waiting and doesn't want to be late for the restaurant (he wants to get away from Celeste as quickly as possible). 8. the Paradise Restaurant.

What Do You Think? 1. a male chauvinist. 2. kind and thoughtful (she doesn't like Arthur but won't hurt his feelings). 3. he didn't have a date with Sabrina. 4. she's afraid Celeste will say something tactless. 5. she said she grew up there with Sabrina. 6. answers will vary (their backgrounds and interests, Celeste, Otto's students, his dog, his life, how he found out who sent the valentine, etc.). 7. that she had a date with Arthur Wolf; unhappy. 8. she hasn't quite figured out that he isn't Arthur Wolf; she's been thinking of him as Arthur all week.

Comparing and Contrasting: 1. Otto likes having her as his supervisor, Arthur hates it. 2. answers will vary (Thursday was a better kite-flying day than Wednesday; Bobby had other things he had to do Wednesday afternoon, etc.). 3. tigers are wild animals and are very large; cats are domestic (tame or tamable) and much smaller than tigers. 4. David is probably older than Robin. 5. answers will vary (Anne is more interested in astronomy than Stephen; she enjoys studying more; he has a job and can't spend extra time, etc.). 6. one bag has many expensive items in it, the other has many cheap items. 7. answers will vary (different temperatures; oxygen on Xeon, not on Krypton; cosmic radiation on Krypton, etc.). 8. answers will vary (36B has larger rooms; 36B has a better view from the windows; it's on the sunny side of the building; it's on the side away from the freeway, etc.).

Information, Please: 1. call someone up and ask for a date; go on a blind date; use a computer dating service. 2. answers will vary. 3. a person who is constantly setting up dates for others. 4. a date in which two couples go out together.

What's the Message? b.

Comparing and Contrasting: both involve going out with someone one doesn't know; in a computer date, one has been matched with others by interests, etc., and one usually has a choice of several dates. Answers will vary on preference.

Figurative Language: 1. d. 2. answers will vary (probably c).

Unit 14 — DEAR DIARY

What's in the Story? 1. unhappy. 2. Trang told a story and everyone forgot about Olga. 3. in the Paradise Restaurant (in a fancy restaurant); he saw Otto and Sabrina. 4. he put her in the back of the room and gave her a test. 5. to eat lunch with her. 6. he showed her the right bus to take. 7. yes; Millie told them stories. 8. he has asked them all to dinner.

What Do You Think? 1. she gets happier as she gets to know the other students. 2. she feels she's an outsider; they tend to disregard her. 3. no; answers will vary (because they became friendly; they felt shy, too; they didn't know anything about her and wanted to go slowly in getting to know her; they might have seen her as an intruder into their social group). 4. answers will vary; be sure students can support their own answers: Juli made the first overture to Olga; Tin-Sek helped her get downtown; Trang gave her a kitten; Ahmad and Maria took her to meet Millie; George is driving her to Mr. Fox's and has obviously driven her before. 5. answers will vary (he wanted her to know that other people had trouble with buses, too; he wanted to make her laugh). 6. he knew she needed a replacement for the cat she had left behind. 7. no; she has no more to say about this and she enjoys the class.

8. answers will vary (that he and Ms. Goodwin are engaged).

Understanding Words Through Context. 1. b. 2. d. 3. d. 4. c. 5. d. 6. b. 7. b. 8. b. 9. d. 10. a. 11. c. 12. c. 13. b. 14. c. 15. b. 16. c. 17. a. 18. d. 19. c. 20. a.

Using Context Clues. 1. a. teacher. b. class, corrected, exams, students, supervisor, bulletin board. 2. a. she has had a baby. b. 2nd & 3rd sentences, little hand, hospital, last sentence. 3. a. joined the armed services; in basic training. b. next three years, up early every morning, march, food is terrible, sergeants, officers. 4. a. veterinarian. b. clients, sick, check-ups, owners, barking, meowing. 5. a. taxi driver. b. traffic was terrible, five trips to the airport, tips were great, customers, friendly, talk.

Understanding Words Through Context. 1. answers will vary (one who looks on the bright side of life). 2. answers will vary (one who looks on the dark side of life). 3. answers will vary (expecting things to be bad). 4. an optimist.

Compare and Contrast. answers will vary.

Unit 15 — SCENES FROM A WEDDING

What's in the Story? 1. Otto and Sabrina's wedding day. 2. Otto's best man. 3. 7:30. 4. be the maid of honor. 5. her mother. 6. Sabrina's back yard. 7. she doesn't know anyone except her classmates, Mr. Fox, and Ms. Goodwin and is afraid that people will talk too fast to her in English. 8. waiting for the rest of the crowd. 9. in case of rain. 10. Hawaii.

What Do You Think? 1. happy. 2. answers will vary (probably not; she's upset that her daughter is grown up and starting a home of her own). 3. quietly (she's unhappy about George's laughter). 4. the person officiating at the wedding (minister, priest, judge, etc.); Otto

answers, "I do." 5. he is an important part of their lives, they are an important part of his. 6. answers will vary (he doesn't want them to feel jealous; he is thinking of the other important parts of his life; they are part of the school setting in which he met Ms. Goodwin, etc.).

Comprehension Review. 1. a. 2. c. 3. c. 4. c. 5. b. 6. d. 7. c. 8. The best things in life are free. 9. 10. a. Get dressed neatly . . . b. Arrive on time . . . c. Answer interview questions . . . d. Before leaving, thank . . . e. Write a letter . . . 11. a. O. b. O. c. F. d. F. 12. a. 13. a. 14. a and c. 15. c.

Information, Please. 1. it is bad luck for the groom to see the bride in her gown before the wedding. 2. from days when marriages were arranged by parents. 3. answers will vary. 4. answers will vary (rabbit's foot, four-leaf clover, horseshoe, etc.). 5. people needed explanations for happenings.

Drawing Conclusions. c.

Understanding Words Through Context. 1. b. 2. b. 3. d.

Understanding Proverbs. a.